21
DAYS TO

Decode
Your
**Dreams**

# Also in the 21 Days series

HAY
HOUSE

CONNECT WITH

# HAY HOUSE

ONLINE

🌐 hayhouse.co.uk          𝐟 @hayhouse

📷 @hayhouseuk          🐦 @hayhouseuk

▶ @hayhouseuk          ♪ @hayhouseuk

Find out all about our latest books & card decks • Be the first
to know about exclusive discounts • Interact with our authors
in live broadcasts • Celebrate the cycle of the seasons with us
• Watch free videos from your favourite authors •
Connect with like-minded souls

'The gateways to wisdom and knowledge
are always open.'

**Louise Hay**

**21 DAYS TO**

# Decode
# Your
# Dreams

Unlock the Signs, Symbols, and

Meanings of Your Dreams

## LEON NACSON

**HAY HOUSE**

Carlsbad, California • New York City

London • Sydney • New Delhi

**Published in the United Kingdom by:**
Hay House UK Ltd, The Sixth Floor, Watson House,
54 Baker Street, London W1U 7BU
Tel: +44 (0)20 3927 7290; www.hayhouse.co.uk

**Published in the United States of America by:**
Hay House Inc., PO Box 5100, Carlsbad, CA 92018-5100
Tel: (1) 760 431 7695 or (800) 654 5126; www.hayhouse.com

**Published in Australia by:**
Hay House Australia Pty Ltd, 18/36 Ralph St, Alexandria NSW 2015
Tel: (61) 2 9669 4299; www.hayhouse.com.au

**Published in India by:**
Hay House Publishers India, Muskaan Complex,
Plot No.3, B-2, Vasant Kunj, New Delhi 110 070
Tel: (91) 11 4176 1620; www.hayhouse.co.in

A catalogue record for this book is available from the British Library.

Tradepaper ISBN: 978-1-78817-906-5
E-book ISBN: 978-1-78817-919-5
Audiobook ISBN: 978-1-78817-861-7

Interior illustration: 12: Lucy Webster

Printed in Great Britain by Clays Ltd, Elcograf S.p.A.

# Contents

# Publisher's Note

Research has shown that establishing a habit requires 21 days of practice. That's why Hay House has decided to adapt the work of some of its most prestigious authors into these short, 21-day courses, designed specifically to develop new mastery of subjects such as decoding dreams.

*21 Days to Master Decoding Your Dreams* draws from Leon Nacson's best-selling *A Stream of Dreams* (Hay House, 2004).

Other titles that will help you to further explore the concepts featured in the 21-day program are listed in the beginning of this book.

# Author's Note

In order to decode your dreams, you need to be able to remember them. I therefore recommend that you keep a recording device, such as your cellphone, by your bed, so that you can record your dreams by retelling them immediately after you wake up. (If your phone does not have the facility to record voices, check on the Internet to see if you can download an app that can do this.) If you do use a cellphone, ensure that it's switched off—nothing interrupts a wonderful night's sleep more than our smartphones. You may prefer to jot down your dreams in a notebook (your Dream Journal), or type them up on your computer. Whichever method you use, the important thing is to ensure that you record your dreams as soon as you awaken in the morning. It's important to recount the dream in the first person as accurately and in as much detail as possible, using phrases such as "I am...," "I feel...," "I hear...," and "I desire..." to help you experience the dream in the moment and capture the emotions.

# Introduction

Why do we dream? The truth is that all forms of research, both scientific and intuitive, are still in the process of working this out. All I'm certain of is that if it wasn't a useful and vital experience, we would have stopped dreaming thousands of years ago. Once we came down from the trees, we got rid of our tails and our extra thumb. When we needed to chase food, we developed longer legs. The point I'm making is that through adaptation we got rid of any organs, body parts, or bodily functions that no longer served us in everyday life. Surely we would have done the same with dreams if they didn't serve a useful purpose?

Everything that you're about to read is my personal hypothesis. These thoughts and perceptions have been critiqued by thousands of individuals who have either read my books, or seen me at live events or in the media. I have had the good fortune to work with some of the leading lights in the field of personal growth and self-empowerment. They have had an enormous influence on my work and what I'm presenting here in this book. I like to call myself a dream coach because I'm not interested in interpreting or analyzing people's dreams *for* them. Rather, I'm writing this book to ensure that within 21 days you'll have all the tools you need to decode your own dreams.

I've also deliberately left out the scientific background on sleep, how often we dream, and information about rapid-eye-movement (REM) sleep and brainwave patterns, because scientific data changes constantly—for example, new research suggests that we do, in fact, dream continuously outside the REM sleep phase, even though it was generally accepted until recently that we only dreamed during REM. What I find particularly interesting is that one could conclude from the latest research that a lot of our dreams are there simply as entertainment—to keep us asleep while our bodies recuperate and repair themselves. After all, if you were minding children and you wanted to keep them occupied while you went about your work in the background, it's likely you would either put on a film or turn on a television program to capture their attention. So, what if a lot of our dreams are merely distractions to keep us quiet and fast asleep while our bodies rejuvenate themselves? It's an interesting premise.

But enough of science and back to dream coaching… I am like any other coach, whether it's in music, sport, or acting. We can give you the basic skills, but it's up to you—the student—to play in tune, kick that goal, or recall the right lines on stage. I believe that the best dream dictionary you will ever read is the one you compile yourself, so what follows is my "coaching manual" for dreamers. The purpose of this information is to inspire you to interpret your dreams easily and to your own satisfaction. (However, please note that anyone who has painful recurring dreams or dreams that are medically related should not try to interpret the dreams themselves, but should instead seek professional advice.)

Dream on, my friends...

# DAY 1

# The Language of Dreams

Before we can start to decode the meaning of our dreams, we first need to be able to understand their language, which is our topic for today. And here's the good news—this will be the easiest language you'll ever learn because you are the creator, the editor, and the proofreader of the language of your dreams.

One of my favourite sayings is "A picture paints a thousand words." If you accept this, you have accepted the reason why we dream in symbols. When we're awake, symbols are universal, immediately recognizable, and easily communicated. Anyone on the planet knows that if they see a cross, or a Star of David, or a crescent moon on top of a building, the sign denotes a place of worship for Christians, Jews, and Muslims respectively. If you see a golden, archlike "M" on the high street, you instantly recognize the logo of a global fast-food chain and know you could get some takeaway food there. If you come across the symbol of a large tick on billboards, you immediately realize it represents a famous brand of sportswear and sneakers. We can grasp the significance of a symbol in a second, whereas it takes much longer to comprehend written words describing exactly the same thing.

When we're awake, we have the facility of rational thought. While sleeping, we prefer to use a type of visual, artistic language to express ourselves because images have the unique ability to satisfy all our five senses at once. When we are in the dream state, it's economical to use an image to describe a situation— similar to opting to watch the movie rather than to read the book.

As with any language, it takes time and effort to understand and translate the symbols in our dreams. And just as our spoken languages evolve over time, so do the meanings of the symbols in dream language. For example, if someone sent you spam in the 70s, it would have been a can of processed meat; these days, receiving spam is related to technology and means finding unwanted e-mails in your inbox. Similarly, if you heard a "tweet" years ago, there would have been a feathered friend nearby; today it means a personal status update on a social networking site.

In the language of dreams, there are few truly universal symbols because every symbol has subjective meaning. Let's take a common symbol like an apple. Imagine in a dream you saw a young maiden hand you a big, juicy apple. If you are a religious person, the symbol may represent forbidden fruit, temptation—and the possibility that you're going to get kicked out of somewhere really nice very soon. For many of us, the apple would be related to a desire to have someone give us an iPhone, an iPad or perhaps a shiny new Mac computer. Then again, maybe the symbolism could be all about inspiration. An apple hit Sir Isaac Newton on the head and he worked out that whatever goes up must come down. Or it may be that the maiden who gave you the apple is warning you that you are hanging around with a dubious individual—"one bad apple spoils the bunch." Perhaps someone is "rotten to the core"... So there can be a big difference in meaning between a symbol that you see when you are awake and the same symbol that appears in your dreams. When we're awake we have the good fortune to be able to use words to accompany the symbol, so that we can make its meaning crystal clear. But since the language in dreams is based purely on symbolism, the meaning associated with the symbol varies from individual to individual.

Dream language and its symbols also change constantly according to what is happening in your waking life. A perfect example is the symbol of a police officer. If you dreamed about the officer on the day you got a ticket for a traffic infringement, you would probably feel that your dream was about poor decision-making and diminishing finances.

However, if you dreamed about the same officer after you'd walked home through a deserted park at night, you'd be more likely to interpret the dream as being about security and protection: same policeman, two different interpretations depending on what had occurred recently while you were awake. No matter what dream dictionaries say about an image you saw in a dream, I strongly advise you to create your own interpretation. The dream image is only as useful as it is meaningful to you at the time it appears.

Dreams have a very powerful ability to solve the everyday dilemmas we face between our conscience and the need to survive and achieve. Let's look at a simple example. Say you are running late one morning and you need to get to work on time. The coffee is brewing away, but you discover there's only a little bit of milk left at the bottom of the carton. What should you do? You decide to use up the milk and rush off to work. Part of you feels guilty because someone else in the house will now have to go out and buy more milk before they can have their morning coffee. But you justify your action by telling yourself that your need takes priority and, of course, you can't afford to be late for work. Perhaps you forget all about this incident during the day—on the surface it's no big deal—but that night your dreams offer their own solutions to rebalance the situation. You see imagery in which you are milking lots of cows and you're surrounded by buckets of milk. Everyone who lives in the house with you carries buckets of it away and starts bathing in it. This dream image helps you to resolve your guilt by emphasizing that the milk you used up was not the last drop of milk in the world. The presence of milk in the dream also reminds you to buy extra milk on your next shopping trip. And finally, the dream suggests that you wake up a little bit earlier— the symbol of cows is one of animals that rise early and need to be attended to almost at the break of dawn.

Once you get into the habit of decoding your dreams, you will be amazed at how good they are at counterbalancing waking events in this way. Look out for such balancing experiences and symbols in your dreams, especially when you know you've done something unthoughtful or out of character in your waking life, as the dreams will remind you to make amends.

# DAY 2

# Emotions

Today we're going to explore a topic that is fundamental to the interpretation of dreams—our emotions. It's often difficult to find the time to truly sit down and appreciate our emotions in the rush of everyday life. Yet, at night, we get the opportunity to slow down, to sleep, and to dream. And it's in our dreams—and the change in rhythm of our minds— that we often tap into the emotions that may have been trying unsuccessfully to get our attention during the day.

Einstein said, "Imagination is more important than knowledge." When it comes to dreaming, I believe that emotions are certainly more important than the knowledge we can acquire from our dreams. Identifying the emotions that pop up in our dreams provides a wonderful opportunity to connect with how we feel, and so better understand where we're at and what is happening in our lives. Our dreams may reflect difficult times but, equally, they can reflect joy and happiness.

So what exactly is an emotion? Most of us have an intuitive sense of what an emotion is, but let's get a true definition. The Merriam-Webster dictionary defines emotion as "a conscious mental reaction, subjectively experienced as strong feeling, usually directed toward a specific object...." Feelings, on the other hand—though the words are often used interchangeably—commonly describe the sensate experience of the emotion: *feeling* sad, angry, joyful, fearful, and so on. Put simply, an emotion is a state of feeling, and a feeling is the sensate experience of the emotion. Phew!

I am fascinated by the approach to the classification of emotions put forward by the theorist Robert Plutchik in 1980, even though it can be regarded as simplistic. He suggested that there are eight primary emotions: joy, acceptance, surprise, fear, sorrow, disgust, expectancy, and anger, and that all other emotions are made up of different combinations of these.

It's not surprising, then, that we often feel confused when we are emotional, which is why it's important to ask yourself: "What exactly am I feeling?" when you wake up from a dream. To assist you, on the next page there are eight faces showing the eight primary emotions that form the basis of identifying the feelings we have while dreaming. (Facial expressions were used to identify emotions as far back as 1884, when William James identified them as behavioral changes.)

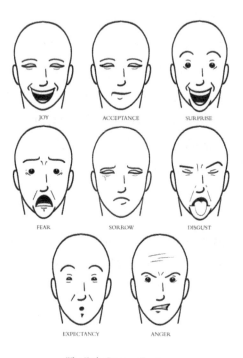

JOY     ACCEPTANCE     SURPRISE

FEAR     SORROW     DISGUST

EXPECTANCY     ANGER

*The Eight Primary Emotions*

When we identify a feeling, we become aware of what brings a particular emotion— joy, peace, wonder, and so on—into our lives. And identifying a particularly difficult emotion can help us to find out what (if anything) we need to do to "work through" it. Often, the best way to work through an emotion is to simply allow it to be, to accept its presence. But it is also often helpful to define the emotion and to grasp what it actually means. For example, if you are feeling jealous, it's helpful to know that jealousy is intolerance of a perceived rivalry or advantage. You can then explore the feeling in the context of the dream by asking yourself what might have triggered it. By getting in touch with the emotion in this way, you can often discover the reason behind the emotion.

It's helpful to remember that every so-called negative emotion has the potential to be a positive one. An emotion is only energy. Like a magnet, with positive and negative ends, we all have a mixture of positive and negative emotions. We don't judge each end of the magnet as good or bad; similarly, it's counterproductive to judge an emotion as good or bad.

To help you work better with the emotions that accompany your dreams, I encourage you to spend a few minutes each morning to sit and think about them before you get up. Often, we're not quite sure how to label or define a feeling or an emotion. To assist you, I suggest that you familiarize yourself with the alphabetical list of commonly experienced emotions, below. Sometimes, we can't identify an emotion because it is a blend of two or more feelings. For example, if you see yourself not getting the job that you were hoping for, you may feel anger, disappointment and, at the same time, relief. The emotion you feel is a blend of all your feelings. Use the list in the same fashion as you would approach a buffet: you're not certain of what to eat, so you browse what's offered; then you make your selection and decide what ends up on your plate. By exploring the different combinations of feelings that make up the emotions on the list, you can gain a much better understanding of your own emotions.

Getting in touch with your emotions will help you to clarify your dreams, so that you can center your thoughts and begin your day with insights that bring self-empowerment.

## List of Emotions

| | | |
|---|---|---|
| Acceptance | Disappointment | Irrationality |
| Agitation | Dissatisfaction | Irritation |
| Alertness | Empowerment | Jealousy |
| Altruism | Failure | Joy |
| Ambition | Faithfulness | Judgment |
| Anger | Fear | Lack |
| Anxiety | Flexibility | Laziness |
| Apathy | Forgiveness | Lethargy |
| Arousal | Frigidity | Liberation |
| Attachment | Fulfillment | Loneliness |
| Blessings | Genuineness | Luck |
| Bliss | Gloominess | Lust |
| Boredom | Gluttony | Miserliness |
| Calmness | Gratitude | Moderation |
| Charity | Grief | Modesty |
| Cheerfulness | Guilt | Negativity |
| Clarity | Ignorance | Negligence |
| Compassion | Ill-treated | Obsession |
| Composure | (feeling) | Obstinacy |
| Confidence | Impatience | Optimism |
| Confusion | Innocence | Pain |
| Contentment | Insensitivity | Paranoia |
| Cursed (feeling) | Inspiration | Passion |
| Depression | Intuition | Patience |
| Detachment | Invincibility | Pessimism |

| | | |
|---|---|---|
| Pity | Sadness | Tension |
| Pleasure | Secretiveness | Thoughtfulness |
| Positive feelings | Selfishness | Trust |
| Praise | Self-pity | Vagueness |
| Protection | Serenity | Vanity |
| Rationality | Sin | Victimization |
| Reassurance | Strength | Vulnerability |
| Relaxation | Success | Weakness |
| Resentment | Suspicion | Worry |
| Respect | Teariness | Worthlessness |

# DAY 3

# Popular Expressions

Today we're going to look at how popular expressions appear in our dreams. No matter what language we speak, we all use popular expressions, metaphors, and anecdotes to assist in getting our message across. It's often much easier to make a point if there is a thought-provoking statement or a humorous story attached to what we're trying to convey. The Scottish poet and writer Robert Louis Stevenson said, "Don't write merely to be understood. Write so that you cannot possibly be misunderstood." That advice is perfect for our waking life, but unfortunately we hardly ever write anything down in dreams. Instead, as we saw on Day 1, we use images because it's far easier and quicker to grasp pictures than words. However, the price we pay for using imagery is that we can misinterpret it, as symbols can be viewed in many different ways. One particularly useful tool that can help us to decipher the symbols in our dreams is to consider whether they are literally visual representations of popular expressions.

Let's take a look at an example. In a dream you see yourself covered in dirt. By running through some popular expressions you may be able to quickly work out why you appeared in this state. Let's say we dismiss the obvious—that you didn't have time to shower before you went to bed and you were actually feeling dirty. You could start by thinking about whether you have been given a difficult or unpleasant task by someone and you feel you got the "dirty end of the stick." Or could it be that someone has "done the dirty" on you, or that you have misrepresented someone and done the dirty on them? Or then again, it may be that you are a little lazy or you've been neglecting your garden and it's time to "get your hands dirty." Or do you feel that someone is currently being dishonest, unfair, or not acting appropriately? If so, ask yourself, "Is someone 'playing dirty' with me?" If you see yourself and all your clothes covered in dirt, it could be an indication that someone is passing on personal information about you or your family—they are talking about things that should be kept within a small group and should never go public. Therefore, you may feel that someone is "washing your dirty linen in public."

I hope you are now getting the idea of how popular expressions can appear in a literal way in dreams. Let's do one more to make sure that we all understand the value of popular expressions and how they relate to dreams.

Let's imagine you saw a vinyl record in your dream. This would be really unusual in this age of downloadable music. It seems such a long time ago that we used to buy our music on vinyl or even on CDs. These days, downloading our favorite tunes is so much simpler and more convenient. The record in the dream could have career implications if you are a DJ— it could be telling you that you're out of touch. But for the rest of us, it could mean many different things, so we'll try referring to some popular expressions. For example, it could be that you want something to be noted and recorded as a true fact—that you have a desire to put something "on the record." Or perhaps it signifies a wish to keep things private between you and a small group of trusted individuals—publicly you have an opinion that you need to stick to for certain reasons, but privately you have a different opinion, so you confide in them "off the record." Or it may be that recently some injustice has been done to you. You know the truth and this particular situation is annoying you. You are hesitant to act because you feel there could be more repercussions, but your dream is telling you to "set the record straight." Finally, do you have a desire to achieve something and be recognized for it? This could be in the field of sport or endurance, knowledge, or creativity. If so, perhaps you have a desire to hold a "world record."

By using "dirt" and "record" as examples of symbols that come up in dreams, we can see that there is a huge range of potential interpretations, feelings, and conclusions that we can come to if we search for popular expressions.

When decoding your dreams it's very important not to be bound solely by the language you speak in your everyday waking life. Because of the Internet, movies, and television programs, popular expressions from many different languages and countries seep into our everyday experiences. For example, most of us have come across *bon appétit*, a French phrase we use to wish our fellow diners enjoyment of their meal; and "hitting a home run," an American baseball term used globally to describe someone who is having a successful streak. Anyone who has an ethnic background should be particularly aware of foreign expressions that they may have heard from their parents or grandparents. I come from a Mediterranean background and my grandparents always used to say, "*L'occhio del padrone ingrassa il cavallo*," which, translated from the Italian, means "The eye of the owner fattens the horse." This indicates to me that if I keep a close eye on my business and my relationships, they will grow larger and stronger. So, if I see a skinny horse in my dream, it tells me that I'm not paying enough attention to my business affairs or to my family and friends.

Through exploring popular expressions, idioms and metaphors, we can reveal so much more than the obvious. This makes them very useful tools in our quest to decode our dreams.

# DAY 4

# Dreams Are Like Onions

I've often said that onions are not only my favorite vegetables, but they are also perfect representations of dreams. Today we are going to look at how we can "peel back" the layers of our dreams to reveal their hidden messages.

The beauty of an onion is that each of its layers is as important as the one above it or below it. Unlike the avocado, which has a big, inedible seed in the center, or corn that not only gets stuck in your teeth but also leaves you with a husk that you can't eat, onions (apart from the outer skin) are appetizing and delicious through to the core.

Just like peeling an onion, decoding a dream involves exploring many layers, and if you're willing to go deep enough, you'll get to the juicy center and discover a lot about yourself. It's important to know that the various layers of a dream never follow a particular order, so what you first think is probably an outer layer can eventually turn out to be at the center. As with the content of dreams, there is no apparent logic to the layers (at least in the waking sense of the word "logic"), but that is what makes decoding them so rewarding.

Generally, the easiest layer of a dream to decode is one that portrays something you did or that happened to you recently in waking life. For example, you may have watched a television program or a movie, or listened to the radio before you went to bed. If so, something relating to this is the most obvious scenario you're going to replay in your dreams. Fall asleep watching a talent show for singers, and you're likely to be auditioning in front of the judges in your dreams.

Or if you doze off when the news is on and a flood or a cyclone is featured, it would not be unusual to dream about extreme weather during the course of the night.

Another very important dream layer usually depicts the emotions you experienced during the day or just before you went to bed. You might have gotten into an argument with a family member or a friend, or you might have had a difference of opinion with a work colleague, and so felt angry in your dream. Or if you had just made a huge sale or been advised of big promotion, you might have had a very joyful dream. Whatever happens in real life, you can expect to replay portions of your experiences and feelings during sleep.

There is also a dream layer that is affected by physical ailments or illness. When you are sick or in pain, the discomfort associated with your physical condition will manifest in some way in your dreams and any discomfort will be integrated into the dream. For example, if you have stomach pains, you might dream that someone hits a ball at your stomach.

One of the reasons why we dream is thought to be to manufacture memory. So, on the memory layer, we are filing away what will be useful for our survival, evolution, and personality, and discarding everything that we don't need. This is no different to the e-mail on your computer—lots of information comes in during the day, you deal with it, and then either store it in the right place or delete it because it is spam or of no further use.

When you try to decode images in this layer, it is important to realize that you are manufacturing memory. Here's an example: say you went to the zoo in waking life and saw a pride of lions in an enclosure surrounded by a moat and an electric fence. You also came across a friendly domestic cat wandering freely around the grounds. It would be natural to see lions, tigers, and other wild cats in your dreams that night, mixed in with their domestic cousins. Processing the information, your mind comes to the conclusion that big cats equal danger (they were fenced in with high security), so it's best to keep away from them, whereas small cats (like the one that rubbed itself against your legs) are cute and cuddly, so they are safe to approach—maybe you should even get one. This is really over-simplifying the way in which the mind works when we're asleep, but I wanted to give you a simple example to follow. So remember, not all symbols need to be interpreted; you could just be manufacturing memory.

Returning to the dream layers, I believe there is also one that concerns itself with boosting our survival techniques. We often see challenges and obstacles in our dreams and more often than not they should be treated like a computer game. When you first play the game, you find it difficult, and the computer beats you every time. But the more you play it, the better you get, and soon you are beating the computer. So, these types of dreams don't need to be interpreted because the mind is generating them to develop our survival skills, and to give us more self-determination and confidence.

The deeper we go into our dreams, the more interesting the layers become. There is one that deals with relationships. On this layer there is no such thing as "thought crime." You should not feel guilty about the scenarios that you experience here—for example, you may find yourself with inappropriate partners, or you may be falling out with your loved ones. No matter what occurs on this level, it's a role-playing exercise to ensure that when you wake up and find you need to deal with an issue, you will have considered it already while you were asleep. This can help you make the most appropriate decisions in real life.

Another important dream layer is the one in which we try to solve problems. We've all heard the expression "Let's sleep on it." This is because we actually do try to work out everything from our most perplexing challenges to where we should go on our next vacation while we're asleep. It's been well documented that Einstein solved the theory of relativity through a dream; the sewing machine was invented from a dream; and the lyrics and tunes of some of our greatest musical hits, such as Paul McCartney's *Yesterday*, have come from dreams. If you're fortunate enough to recall your dreams when you're in this layer, you can solve things in the most creative ways and come up with some truly inspirational ideas and inventions. My advice is, as soon as you wake up from this layer, go straight to the patents and trademark office and register whatever you saw!

We now get to the wish-fulfillment layer, where we dream of our highest aspirations and desires. At this level everything can be fixed without any ramifications—it's impossible to gain weight here or to be undesirable. We're full of wisdom and so young, healthy, and blessed with abundance that we just never want to wake up. This layer is very important because it's where seeds are planted in our imagination—and it's our imagination that adds meaning to our lives.

When we reach the core of our dreams—the center of the onion—we are receiving messages directly from our higher self, without any ego, baggage, negativity from past events, or fear of what could happen tomorrow getting in the way. You will know that you have arrived there because it's the place where you feel totally centered, and full of love and pure potentiality.

# DAY 5

# How to Decode Your Own Dreams

Over the past few days we have examined some of the key components of dream decoding, so today we are going to look at how to approach the actual process of interpreting our dreams.

I love the biblical quote, "Physician, heal thyself," because it could apply to dream decoding. Dreamer, understand yourself. When it comes to exploring dreams there is no better dream interpreter than you, yourself. I recommend that we put all our dream dictionaries in a recycling bin, so that the recyclers find a better use for the paper. You may think this is very strange coming from a person who has written numerous books on dreams. Here is the difference: conventional dream dictionaries try to do the same job as a language dictionary. For example, they tell you very clearly that steel is a hard metal used in construction; there's no ambiguity in that. But if you saw steel in a dream, it could mean that someone is stealing from you, that someone is sneaking around, or a host of other things. While words can be defined in a dictionary, symbols cannot be pinned down in the same way because their interpretation, like the appreciation of beauty, is totally subjective and unique to the dreamer.

I believe it's very important to record dreams. Some of us love writing or typing, and it's fine to keep a Dream Journal by your bedside or on your computer. But if you're like me, you might find it easier to use a recording device. These days, with all the fabulous smartphones around, it's so simple to download an app that will not only record everything you say, but even transcribe it for you for later downloading. By recording your dreams in this fashion rather than writing them down, you can also incorporate feelings and emotions into the way you articulate what happened, which will help you in the decoding process. In addition, it's very convenient because you don't need to wake up your partner by turning on the bedside light to write something down, and then try to get back to sleep. But of course, use whatever method suits you best. The important thing is to make sure that you record your dreams regularly.

Each morning, upon waking, answer the following questions and record your answers:

- What time did I go to bed?

- What did I eat before I went to bed?

- What did I drink?

- What did I watch, read, or listen to?

- What mood was I in?

- Did I take any medication? If so, what was it?

- What was on my mind as I was trying to go to sleep?

The dreams that you have recorded and the answers to the above questions will assist you greatly in decoding your dreams. They will also help you to see if there are any common factors affecting your dreams. You will notice from the questions that I also think it's important to keep a record of what happened in the hours before you fell asleep. For example, you might discover that every time you have tea and a chocolate biscuit just before bed you don't recall any dreams at all, but if you simply have the tea, dreams seem to flood back to you.

We're now ready to take a look at the way that I, from the point of view of a dream coach, suggest you decode a dream. We start by looking at the feelings that appear in the dream; then we consider any relevant popular expressions that might come to mind and assess what the important dream layers appear to be.

Let's begin with the following dreams and work on them together.

## Dream 1

*I was asked to be a part of band and become the lead singer. I was excited, but I didn't think my voice was good enough. The strange thing was that they asked me to sing in Greek. I was also concerned that I hadn't got enough money to pay for my costumes. Everyone involved supported me, but I still felt inadequate.*

**Feelings:** Unconfident; included; accepted; excited; supported; inadequate

**Popular expression:** "It's all Greek to me"

**Layers (of the onion):** Finances; wanting to be in the lead or the center of attention

### Dream Coach's feedback:

This dream is about self-esteem. It's telling you to be more confident in yourself. By developing new confidence, you will find more work, earn a greater income, and so help resolve your financial problems. Start off with being part of the team and resist your urges to control everything. Also, this dream is telling you to study, because whatever now seems incomprehensible ("all Greek") to you will start to make sense once you learn and understand more about it.

## Dream 2

*Lately, I often seem to be dreaming about death— whether my own, or that of a friend or a stranger. In this dream I myself died and the thing I remember most is a disturbing image of a worm coming out of my ring finger.*

**Feelings:** anxious, sense of loss, fearful, surprised

**Popular expressions:** "to worm out of"; "a can of worms"

**Dream layers:** endings; change; partnerships

### Dream Coach's feedback:

This dream is about endings and a desire for new beginnings. You are experiencing fear around losing family and friends because of a decision that you want to make. After anything is destroyed, something new is always created. Because the worm came out of your ring finger, it may be that you want to "worm out of" a marriage or a close relationship, which will in turn open up "a can of worms" affecting family and friends.

I can guarantee that if you follow this approach and apply your own individual creativity to interpreting your dreams, my job as coach will be done and there will be a gold medal waiting for you!

# DAY 6

# The Elements

As human beings, in spite of all our physical and cultural diversity, we all belong to the same race. It is therefore unsurprising that a few dreams are common to us all and form part of our collective consciousness. Today we are going to consider one of the most prevalent universal symbols: the elements.

Traditionally, the elements are made up of water, fire, air, and earth.

## Water

I don't think I've met anyone who hasn't had a water dream, whether the element appeared in its usual liquid form, as a vapor such as mist, or as a solid, such as ice or snow. The first thing to consider when decoding a dream about water is that you may be dehydrated, either literally (physically) or metaphorically (spiritually). Drinking more water will help you to quench a physical thirst, but quenching a spiritual thirst isn't as easy. Are you feeling dissatisfied with your life? If so, why? How can you assuage this thirst?

Water is a universal symbol that relates to emotions: the ebb and flow of life, and the waxing and waning of the moon. (The moon influences all water—including the high water content of our bodies—just as it does the ocean tides.) If life is smooth sailing, you're likely to see still waters in your dreams. But during times of emotional turmoil, it's common to dream of tidal waves and/or rough seas. If we replace the word "water" with the word "emotion," it speaks volumes. For example, if you dream of stormy waters, ask yourself if you're also experiencing tempestuous emotions in waking life.

When water appears as a mist in a dream, it may indicate that you're not seeing things clearly. Is something or someone clouding your vision? What emotional experience is blinding you to reality? Mist is dissolved by sunlight and warmth. If you're feeling melancholy, what can you do to dissolve the mood and cheer yourself up? If you dream of ice, is your mind alluding to "frozen" feelings? What will help you "defrost" these emotions? And if a large amount of snow appears in your dream, you could be feeling overwhelmed or "snowed under," perhaps with work or simply too much going on in your life. Snow is also a symbol of individuality, as all snowflakes are unique.

Over the years I've noticed an increase in the number of people who have dreams of water sports. These dreams speak of competition and a desire to feel and conquer emotions. Diving dreams suggest a willingness to "sink to the depths" of despair to reach the bottom of a painful or fearful emotional experience. The upside is the exhilaration we feel when we re-emerge.

## Fire

After water, the next most popular element to appear in dreams is fire, which is the only element we humans have found impossible to pollute. This is the very reason that fire is used in so many initiation or ceremonial activities of indigenous cultures—to purify.

There's a fascination and a real bond between humans and fire. Many would go so far as to say that, without fire, humans would have died out. Watching an open fire is mesmerizing. Perhaps, as we look into the flames, we can be truly present, and we are able to ask ourselves the three great questions that have haunted humankind since the beginning of time: "Who am I?" "What am I doing here?" and "Where am I going?"

Whenever fires burn in any form during a dream, I always ask the dreamer to consider whether they are going through a rite of passage or a phase of purification in their life. It's a fabulous symbol because after any serious fire, especially in nature, there's always regeneration. Fire can also be a symbol of passion, motivation, and desires that burn deep inside. Is someone "firing you up"? Or do you need to tone down your behavior because you might end up "fired" from your job? Is the fire in your dream warm and inviting? If so, then ask yourself, "What do I need to do to 'add fuel to my fire?'" The answer could be to go back to school, to learn a new skill, or simply to socialize more. On the other hand, do you feel threatened by fire in your dream? If the fire is too hot and uncomfortable, consider cooling things down in your life. Perhaps take up meditation, try Tai Chi, or take a relaxing vacation.

## Air

For an element that we can't see, air certainly plays an enormous part in our very existence. Depending on its mood, air can be welcoming or frightening, a breath of fresh air or a tornado—the only difference is the speed at which it is traveling. Does the air in your dream indicate that it's time for you to slow down and take a fresh look at your current situation? If so, you will enjoy life a lot more at a more measured pace. If you see gales blowing in your dream, perhaps you feel "blown away" by the challenges around you. If so, it's very important not to forget your "second wind"— once you've composed yourself, you can literally start over and hopefully go on to accomplish your original goal. At some point in our lives we need to put our intellect aside and go with our gut feeling. The wind that you feel in your dream could be asking you to "throw all caution to the wind."

## Earth

Our planet supports everything, even the water-bound animals. Without solid ground—earth—beneath us we would face a very shaky existence. In your dream, have you got your feet "firmly planted on the ground"? Are you walking confidently? If so, this would indicate that whatever challenges you're facing at the moment, you feel secure that success is at hand.

If the ground is soft or muddy, if you are stumbling and reaching for support, the dream indicates that you haven't laid the proper foundations for whatever you're working on or dealing with. Whatever you're trying to build, whether it's a business, a relationship, or even inner strength, it's time to go back to your original plans, reinforce your commitment, and remind yourself of the reason why you embarked on the project in the first place.

Elemental dreams are very important, especially ones that combine two or more of the elements. Fire, water, air, and earth are all interrelated. For example, there can't be any fire without air, and water can't continue on its never-ending journey without the ground beneath supporting the oceans and the rivers. So when the elements appear in your dreams, take time to consider them, and pay special attention to the symbolism of how the elements interact with one another.

## DAY 7

# Dream Backdrops

I love the word backdrop because it's so important, yet it has no ego. It's there, it enriches the experience, but it doesn't want to take center stage. The backdrop on a stage works with the actors, supports them, and ensures that their performance is enhanced. The same applies to the backdrop, setting, or background of a dream, which is our subject for today.

Dream backdrops improve and enhance the picture so that emotions are very clear and the decoding is more precise. I believe it's very important to spend as much time interpreting the background of a dream as we spend on the symbols. Moreover, on most occasions it is far easier to interpret the background and relate it to an emotion than it is to interpret the symbol.

As you consider the backdrop to your dream, ask yourself the following questions:

- Where was I?

- Have I been there before, or is it somewhere I've never visited?

- Was the dream set in the past, the present, or the future?

- Was I excited or disappointed?

- Was I scared or comfortable?

- Do I want to go back, or do I never wish to return?

It's important to look at all these questions without thinking about who was there and what else you saw. If you can get the background right when decoding a dream, you are well on the way to reaching the right conclusions.

Was the background you saw historical? If so, it could be a past-life dream or an indicator that you're living in the past. We've heard the phrase "the good old days" so many times—when the air was cleaner, things were cheaper, and there were no wrinkles on our foreheads. It's usually a very comfortable place to go to in our dreams because it's very familiar to us. When we wake up from such dreams we feel reassured. If traveling back in time creates an uncomfortable feeling and you feel uneasy, don't be concerned that you are going to relive the past upon waking. We usually have these dreams to ensure that we don't repeat our mistakes. If during our waking life we are encountering the same old problem we've had before, we can expect to travel in our dreams to a time when the problem first occurred, to remind us how much we didn't like it. In almost every case, upon waking, we resolve not to fall into the same trap again.

Usually, if we are dreaming that we're in Antarctica or in some frozen wasteland it means that the quilt has fallen off the bed and, naturally, we're cold. A lot of desert and tropical backgrounds occur when we're all wrapped up in bed, wearing warm pyjamas, with the heating on in the room. In other words, the background climate and weather in our dreams usually relate to the surroundings we're in when we're asleep and our body's desire to get a good night's sleep without waking up. You can test this quite easily by simply leaving a window open one night (assuming it's safe to do so), and you will notice that at some point you will have a dream about the wind blowing, perhaps on the high seas or across an open plain, or in some other scenario that appeals to your imagination.

If you are sure that your dream's backdrop has nothing to do with the room temperature or your choice of bedding, then ask yourself the following questions:

• What storm do I think is brewing?

• Am I making a "storm in a teacup"?

- Am I feeling "under the weather"?

- Am I feeling "snowed under"?

- Is it time to "make hay while the sun shines"?

By answering the above questions you can explore how the symbols, the emotions and the background all relate to each other.

Sometimes our dreams have abstract backgrounds—like a Salvadore Dalí painting—and the scenes either don't make sense or are very surreal. These are non-conformist dreams. They indicate that you have a desire to be challenged and continually inspired. Ask yourself the following questions:

- Who is trying to make me conform?

- What is it in my life that is boring and predictable?

- Why am I excited by strange and bizarre things?

- Do I only feel safe when I'm unpredictable?

Through the answers to these questions you can make some profound discoveries about yourself. Perhaps you are addicted to excitement, or you feel as if you're always out of place, or there's nowhere that you fit in comfortably. Context is paramount here, so it also depends at what stage in your life you have this dream. If it occurs at a time when you're going from being a teenager to an adult or coming to the end of a relationship, it's usual to feel out of place. When it's time for a change, it's normal to feel excited by imagined experiences. It's all about the timing of the dream.

For most of us, dream backgrounds fall into two categories: familiar or unfamiliar. Familiar settings are simple enough—they are usually our workplace, our home, or a much-visited vacation destination. These backgrounds give us comfort and reassure us that everything is fine and in its proper place. They also give us a starting point from which to decode the dream. For example, say you see yourself in your workplace and you keep tripping over for no apparent reason—it's likely you literally "can't stand" where you are working.

It's the unfamiliar backdrops that are more intriguing. If you see yourself falling over in a strange workplace, perhaps it's not a great time to change careers. For example, say you are a struggling musician and you are considering a move into the world of finance. Then, in your dream you see yourself falling over in your local bank. This would mean that it probably wouldn't be advisable to apply for a job in the financial sector right now. If the dream background is somewhere overseas, or somewhere in a city or a town you've lived in or visited, it's important to look very closely at what's happening in the dream. Is your situation comfortable or uncomfortable? Do you wake up feeling successful, or frustrated at underachieving? Did you want to stay there or leave? When you examine your answers to these questions, you will know if it's time for a change. The different backgrounds in dreams are great indicators that it's either time to stay put or time to create a completely different scene.

# DAY 8

# Falling, Flying, and Being Chased

I've often wondered why it's a common human perception that things occur in threes. It may be because we live in a three-dimensional world, and for anything to materialize we need height, width, and length. In dreams, there are three common dimensions of experience: falling, flying, and being chased, which are our topics for today. There are not many of us who haven't experienced at least one of these types of dream, and I dare say most of us have had all three at some time in our lives.

## Falling

Let's start with falling. It's impossible to fall, whether awake or asleep, if you are on solid ground and have sure footing. It is therefore very important to look at your surroundings when you have a dream where you are tumbling down. Ask yourself:

- Am I at home? If so, do I feel unsupported by my family?

- At work? If so, do I feel a lack of support from my work colleagues?

- In a social setting? If so, do I feel undermined by my friends?

- In an unfamiliar setting? If so, do I always feel unsupported?

- On my own? If so, am I guilty of not giving myself enough support?

If you could relate to any of the first three questions on the above list, ask yourself, "Why is the support of this person or these people so important to me?" Often, we don't really need validation from the people around us. We all have individual opinions about certain issues, and it is normal to disagree with our family, colleagues, and friends about some things. After all, it would be a boring world if everyone agreed with each other all the time. However, if the falling dreams continue, the simplest way to stop them is to ask for help from the people whose support you feel you lack.

Unfortunately, it's usually the last scenario on the list that is most prevalent, as many of us unwittingly undermine ourselves. We tend to be very hard on ourselves and have high expectations—we always want to punch above our weight. The good news is that when you see yourself falling in a dream and you know you're guilty of not giving yourself enough support, it's easy to rectify. All you need to do is begin to speak in a kinder way about yourself—for example, stop saying, "I'm such an idiot, I always lose my car keys," or "I just can't remember names," and so on, and begin to say, "I misplace my car keys, but I always manage to find them once I relax and retrace my steps," or "I'm not great with names, but I never forget a face." The more you can bolster yourself in both your inner and outer dialogues, the less you will dream that you are falling.

## Flying

Everything about a flying dream is fabulous. The only downside is that you don't get any frequent flyer points! Flying dreams occur when we need to lift our spirits, when we require an overview of our current situation, or when we need to take a mental vacation. Life can get very mundane, especially between Monday and Friday. Most of us have a set routine; we have to be at a certain place by a certain hour every morning, and we can't leave until a certain time every evening. Humans don't naturally respond well to such regimentation, so through our dreams we have created a way to rise above everyday routine. In a flying dream we can take off and soar above the mundane, lifting our spirits so that we wake up the next morning as fresh and optimistic as possible.

From time to time, we cannot get a true perspective of a situation and we require a birds-eye view. For example, if we wanted to get a view of our suburb, we would take a helicopter ride above it; if we wanted to see our whole city, we would circle high above it in a plane; and if we wanted to understand our planet, we would need to go up into orbit in a spacecraft. The higher the vantage point, the better the view. By elevating ourselves above our challenges we obtain a better idea of the full picture.

It's not always easy to get away when we need to the most, but our dreams allow this to happen in the blink of an eye. In our sleep we can travel to foreign shores, soar over mountains, float over oceans, and hover above the most beautiful and romantic settings imaginable. These dreams leave us invigorated, re-energized, and keep us going until we can get away on a real vacation.

## Being Chased

I love dreams of being chased, yet many people find them terrifying. The reason I enjoy these dreams is that I've realized something very illuminating: usually, the symbol that's chasing me, or that I'm running away from, is none other than *me*. Bearing this revelation in mind, when you dream of being chased, ask yourself the following questions:

• What is it about myself that I can't face?

• What is it that I don't want to catch up with me?

• What is it that I'm running away from?

• Is it time to stop running and make a stand?

We all have skeletons in the closet—we all have experiences, sides of our personality, or incidents that we want to leave behind. (I read somewhere that it's thought that within ten years, most children growing up now will change their names because of all the information that has been posted on Facebook about them. The fear is that a prospective employer or partner will view something these young people did as teenagers and will therefore have concerns about them as adults.) The point is that from time to time our past resurfaces to chase us in our dreams. But, once you can totally accept yourself (including your "shadow" self), along with all the events that have been part of your life's journey, you will stop chasing yourself in your dreams. My good friend Deepak always says, "The only place there's no shadow is in darkness."

Of course, if you're certain the symbol chasing you in your dream is *not* you, you need to find out more. Ask yourself the following questions:

- Who am I running away from?

- What will happen if they catch me?

- What am I avoiding?

- What will happen if I face them?

In the immortal words of Albert Einstein, "Any intelligent fool can make things bigger and more complex... It takes a touch of genius and a lot of courage to move in the opposite direction." If your dream only occurred once, try to work who or what the symbol represented and then move on. But if this dream reoccurs on a regular basis, and using your answers to the questions above, it's time to take positive steps in your waking life to face the fear associated with the dream chase and being caught. The most effective way to do this is to face whatever it is that's chasing you. I've mentioned that usually, and much to our surprise, it is we who are doing the chasing. Once we realize this, we simply need to accept ourselves completely. Self-acceptance and self-support quickly eliminate the fearful things that we're running away from.

# DAY 9

# Teeth, the Body, and Body Parts

Today we are looking at dreams of teeth, and the body and its parts.

## Teeth

One of the most common types of dream reported to me concerns teeth. I'm constantly told of scenarios in which teeth fall out, or they are cracked, or they end up in the dreamer's hands, or the dreamer is desperately trying to put them back in their mouth. Often the gums and the face are swollen and sore, and the dreamer's face is distorted in pain. Because some of us do not maintain our teeth even as regularly as we maintain our motor vehicles, we can experience all sorts of problems in our mouths. And rather than allowing us to wake up in the middle of the night from pain caused by a wobbly filling or an exposed nerve, our mind creates a dream scene that mirrors the physical problem we are experiencing. But if you do wake up with toothache, you won't need help with decoding your dream—you'll be too busy rushing off for treatment.

Sometimes dreams of teeth can be a straightforward depiction of the dreamer's underlying concern about their dental health—I have scarcely met a single individual who hasn't put off a scheduled visit to the dentist at some time or another. The very idea of going to the dentist is often more painful than the treatment. So, if you are not in pain, the next thing to ask yourself is: "When did I last go to the dentist for a check-up?"

Once you have dismissed any connection with a physical problem or concern about your teeth, you can consider some wider meanings. If you're involved in a major project, or trying to start a new relationship, you may dream that your teeth are loose. This type of dream suggests that you're not able to "get your teeth into" the situation.

Another popular dream theme is rotting or weak teeth. This may indicate that you feel as though your youth is slipping away. It could be a vanity issue— appearance counts for a lot in this world, and anything that detracts from our appearance can be upsetting. If you feel overweight or ugly when you are awake, you may dream of rotting teeth.

When your teeth fall out in a dream it can mean that you feel as if you're losing face in some way. In many cultures this indicates embarrassment and being put in a position that lowers your self-esteem, leaving you feeling isolated from others. Think about where you were when your teeth fell out. Was it a family situation or were you at work? What embarrassed you? I've found that the higher-profile an individual is, the more often these dreams occur.

Perhaps you dream that someone else's teeth fall out: your dog, the lady next door, or a family member. If so, you may have concerns about their health or general state of well-being. If it's a dog, you may be worried about the health of a very good friend.

If another person's teeth fall out in a dream, it may relate to an aspect of yourself. For example, if you dream that, say, Sly Stallone's teeth fall out, you may feel that the strong and muscular part of yourself is in decline. If it's a relationship dream—for example, your partner's teeth fall out and he or she is in good health, with no dental problems—it may signify that there are communication problems within the relationship.

## The Body and Its Parts

Now that we've covered the part of our body we dream about most, perhaps we should look at the body as a whole and some of the other parts that help us to function.

When we see a whole body in our dream, the first thing to do is to examine its state. If the body is lifeless, ask yourself, "Is it time for me to take a stand and not weaken in any way, because whatever someone is asking me to do should be 'over my dead body?'" Or could you be concerned about an individual knowing things about you that you do not wish to reveal? If so, perhaps the dream is telling you that this person knows "where the bodies are buried."

In many cultures the body is a living, organic temple to be revered at all times. Is the body in your dream healthy, well maintained, and full of vitality? Or is it exhausted, out of balance, or declining? Throughout the ages, dreams about the body have been the perfect indicator of the dreamer's well-being. Dreams have and will continue to alert us at a very early point if there is an imbalance that needs attention. I highly recommend that you consult a health professional if there is a reoccurrence of any dreams that show your body temple in disrepair. If your temple is vital and in great shape, then continue doing whatever you're doing—you're on the right track.

Over the course of time we have associated parts of our body with emotions: the backbone is linked with courage; the head with thinking; the heart with romance; the stomach with anxiety; and the Achilles heel with vulnerability. Here is the most important point: When trying to decipher a dream that contains a body part as a main component, what is the emotion you associate with that body part? Are you trying to "mend a broken heart"? Is there something you "can't stand"? What can't you "stomach" anymore? Body parts in dreams are pure, definite, and precise indicators of the deep-rooted feelings that we wish to express or expose.

# DAY 10

# Death

We constantly think about our mortality while we're awake, even though most of the time we're not aware of doing this; so it's not really surprising that we also dream about death. This is our topic for today.

Both Mark Twain and Jeff Goldblum said, "The reports of my death are greatly exaggerated." This is so true when you dream of your own death because it obviously didn't happen—you're alive and trying to make sense of it by decoding the dream!

In between canvases, Pablo Picasso said, "Every act of creation is first an act of destruction." This is the foundation for interpreting all dreams about death. What we are in fact seeing is the end of one thing and the beginning of another. We are glimpsing transitions; we are witnessing change. Of course, there have been recorded instances of death dreams being premonitions, but I've deliberately chosen not to delve into these dreams, because I feel they are not within the scope of this book.

Let's accept the hypothesis that a dream about death is really about change. It may be uncomfortable, but it's important to go back into the dream and look at who died. Ask yourself the following questions:

- What was my relationship with that person?

- How close was I to that person?

- Was it a stranger?

- Was I sad or accepting?

- Was there a wake?

- What was I wearing?

Explore the emotions and feelings that surfaced in the dream as deeply as you can, knowing that it may be painful, but there's a purpose. If you saw a family member, a friend, or a colleague die, it could be that your relationship with that person is coming to an end or that you are about to form a different kind of relationship with them. This type of dream occurs frequently when a member of our family or social circle is about to go through a divorce. What we are seeing is the "death" of their relationship and the "birth" of two people going their own ways.

Sometimes, seeing someone's death in a dream can mean that they are going through a mid-life crisis or the menopause. The person is changing completely: in the case of the mid-life crisis they are behaving in a strange manner, their old values disappear, and they have a different view on life. In the case of the menopause, the person is experiencing powerful physical changes that are occurring mainly internally. It's natural to see her dying in your dream, but it's also very important to acknowledge that what you're witnessing is a profound change in her life.

Surely the worst death dream of all is one showing a child passing away. However, this dream usually denotes change, often appearing when the child is growing up or approaching a milestone, such as puberty or adulthood. With puberty, what you are seeing is the "death" of the child and the "birth" of the adolescent. When a young person turns 18, in most countries they are able to vote and to get married without needing permission from their parents. If you dream of someone of this age passing away, you are visualizing the "death" of the adolescent who was so reliant on their parents, and the "birth" of an independent young man or woman. I sincerely hope that this perspective offers some comfort, because it can very difficult to dream of the death of our child and then wake up and allow them to carry on living their life as before—the natural urge is to protect them from all harm. But the mere fact that we are able to act out our worst fears in our dreams may allow us to live our waking lives with less fear.

Feelings and emotions in death dreams are very important. If you felt sad in your dream, were you crying for the dead person or for your own loss? We often feel inadequate and helpless when people are suffering. If the individual whom you saw pass away in the dream is suffering in waking life, and you experience a certain sense of relief and calmness in the dream, you could be fulfilling your wish to relieve their pain.

If you saw yourself dying or dead in a dream, pay really close attention. The first thing, of course, is to review your current state of health and ensure that you make appointments for those check-ups you've been avoiding. You definitely don't need a dream coach to remind you of that. Once they have been attended to, you could ask yourself the following questions:

- How was I remembered?

- Am I going through a mid-life crisis?

- What physical changes are occurring?

- Do I think something is "killing" me?

- What aspect of myself is "dying"?

- What am I "dying" to do?

Seeing yourself dying or dead in a dream is quite a profound experience. Also, it's so exciting because you get to jump out of bed with joy when you wake up and discover it was only a dream! Once you've readjusted to being alive, ask yourself if you want to "kill off" some part of yourself. For example, it may be that you want to stop procrastinating and you've decided to be assertive. It may be that you want to change your career or your relationship and just see your old ways "dead and buried."

Often, we have regrets for all the things we could have and should have done. Is your dream telling you to create a list of places to visit and experiences to have before it's too late? Did you see a tombstone, and if so, what was written on it? Is that how you want to be remembered? Is your dream telling you it's time to change the way you present yourself because you didn't like your eulogy? Was there a wake in your dream? The best death dreams have a wake attached to them—just as we celebrate when someone is born, we should have an equally fine celebration when they have moved on.

Death may seem to be a depressing subject, but, actually, it's about transformation and celebration. I hope this chapter encourages you to think about rebirth and to take time to "smell the roses." As the old saying goes: the past is history, the future is a mystery, and the present is a gift. This adage sits well here because when we see a dream that contains death, it's a reminder to be appreciative of the present and to enjoy every moment. I'll conclude with the beautiful words that Louise L. Hay said to herself while looking in the mirror, "I really, really love you. You are my best friend, and I enjoy living my life with you." I encourage you to do the same each morning.

# DAY 11

# Animals

Wouldn't it be great to be just like Dr. Dolittle and talk to the animals? Humans have over the ages attributed certain traits and characteristics to animals in an attempt to understand them better. Wouldn't you just love to be able to talk with a fox and ask, "Are you really cunning?" or, "What do you think about when you're in your den?" Until we can actually do this, animals will continue to be enigmatic and powerful symbols in our dreams. Today we will explore what our dream animals could mean.

When an animal appears in your dreams, it's important to first consider what it currently represents to you.

For example, say you see a giraffe at a point in your life when you are taking chances on a new business venture. This would be an indication that you feel you are "sticking your neck out" a long way. If you then dream about the same giraffe later, when you have to make unwelcome changes to the business, the animal could indicate that you're finding your position "hard to swallow."

Many indigenous cultures, especially the Native Americans, believe that certain animals are with us throughout our lives as our spirit guides. Does the bird in your dream indicate perhaps that you need to allow yourself to soar like an eagle in your waking life? Or does the dream bear mean that you should "hibernate" for a while and detach yourself from everything until more fruitful times come around again? A bear can represent great power and strength, yet at the same time denote gentleness and a nurturing attitude toward the young. Is there someone around you who is being bullied and looking to you to protect them, just like a mother bear and her cub?

It's important that you take into account your ethnic background when interpreting the dreams. Animals are attributed with different powers depending on what continent they're on. For example, the owl is considered a predator and a bad omen in some parts of the world, such as in Arabia and Jamaica, but wise and learned, and a healer, in other places. In ancient Rome and in most places where the Romans had influence, a physician would hang out a signboard featuring an owl to indicate that treatment was available. In Anglo-Saxon cultures, we often hear the description "as wise as an owl" or that an owl symbolizes knowledge.

No matter what animal you see in your dream, it's important to investigate your feelings toward it. Do you feel frightened, reassured, or a million things in between? One of the best animals to illustrate the importance of feelings in dream interpretation is the dog.

Dogs are a great symbol of unconditional love. They will follow you to the ends of the Earth and wait for you no matter how long you are away. Does the dog in your dream indicate that you wish your family, friends, or co-workers would accept you just the way you are?

Obviously, if you own a dog and it appears in your dreams, you don't need a dream coach to explain the meaning. However, when you appear to have an unfamiliar dog in your dream, the symbol deserves a lot of attention.

First, look at the breed of dog. For example, is it a German Shepherd, a French Poodle, or an Irish Setter? If it is from a breed that is identified with a particular country or part of the world, your dream could be letting you know that you have a particular affinity with that country or area. Deep down, you may feel a bond with the culture or a sense of friendship with the people of that place. The dog in the dream could therefore represent your ideal travel destination.

Does the dog in your dream feel aggressive or protective? This can indicate the level of vulnerability or assurance that you are currently feeling in waking life. If the dream dog is aloof and unfriendly, you might think that your best friend is not being supportive; but if the dog in your dream is cuddling up to you, you're more likely to believe that you can count on them.

What are you and the dog doing in the dream? Are you working or playing? Is the animal appearing because you feel overworked and underpaid, and you're "working like a dog." If you're playing with the dog, it could indicate that it's time to get out and enjoy nature. Or, if you see the pooch sitting in its kennel, perhaps the dream is telling you that you're "in the dog house" in your waking life.

I've used a dog as an example to make it easy, and because it's an animal we can all relate to, but you can use the same method to interpret the meaning of any animal you see in your dreams. Whether it's an aardvark or a zebra, whether it's domesticated or wild, explore the characteristics you believe the animal has, your current feelings toward that animal, any ethnic connections, any expressions that mention it, how it's reacting to you and how you're reacting to it.

By following this process, you can gradually reveal the significance of any animals you see in your dreams.

# DAY 12

# Family and Children

Today we are going to examine the meaning of family and children in our dreams.

As Harper Lee's character Atticus says in *To Kill a Mockingbird*, "You can choose your friends but you sho' can't choose your family…." But here's another truth: in most cases our family is all we have. This means that dreaming of family members could be symbolic of doing the best we can with whatever we've got.

It's very rare to see the whole family together in our dreams—as rare as it is when we're awake. Such family gatherings usually only take place on big occasions, such as landmark birthdays, weddings, and funerals. So when everyone shows up together in a dream, it's also a big occasion.

To help you analyze the significance of this dream, ask yourself the following questions:

- Did I feel I was invited to the gathering, or did I just turn up?

- Was I the center of attention, or did I go unnoticed?

- Was I happy or sad?

- Did everyone get along, or were there arguments?

- Did I feel respected or marginalized?

With the aid of your answers, you will gain a better understanding of how you currently feel about your family relationships. This type of dream can also indicate whether or not it's time for you to make an effort to reconnect with your family, as you could be feeling that you're drifting apart. However, equally, after seeing them all in your dream, you might feel there's no need to catch up with them until the next big family occasion.

In any dream about your family, it's important to explore whether you felt part of the family unit or felt like an outsider. Ask yourself the following:

- Why did I feel comfortable or uncomfortable?

- Who included me?

- Who excluded me?

- Are they still stuck in the past?

- Is someone overly competitive?

- Is someone still bullying me?

- Have I changed since our last contact?

These reflections will enable you to understand what is stopping you from enjoying the family environment. (Bear in mind, too, that the dream family could represent your colleagues or your social circle—after all, these are all different types of "families" and your dream could be disguising one "family" as another.)

If your dreams included extended family members, again it's essential to ask yourself all the questions listed above and to determine how you feel about the relationships you have with this larger group. Extended families are interesting because they include people who weren't born into that particular family but who, instead, have joined by becoming the partners of people in it. It's important to remember here that it works both ways. You didn't choose them and they didn't choose you, but now you are all in the same clan together. This is a great symbol of live and let live.

While it is rare to dream of the whole family at once, it is common to dream of individual family members, such as siblings, parents, uncles, and aunts. When a member of the family enters your dream, ask yourself the following:

- Was I happy to see them or annoyed?

- How did they greet me?

- How did I greet them?

- Did they have something to tell me?

- Did I have something to tell them?

- Have they passed on or are they still alive?

Once you've taken the time to process your feelings about meeting this person in your dream, you can then decide if it's important to connect with them in waking life.

Parents and grandparents in dreams usually appear to teach us something we need to reinforce or to remind us how similar we are to them. We often deny that we are just like our mothers and fathers but as the years go by, we do tend to take on many of their views and values. That is frequently pointed out in our dreams.

When our siblings appear in our dreams they usually represent unresolved issues from our waking lives. Our feelings about our brothers and sisters can vary from one extreme to the other: competitive or supportive, disappointed or proud. In normal families and in our dreams, there is usually the whole range of different feelings or a combination of everything we just described. Our dreams help us sort out the unfinished business, the unsaid, in the hope that it will make the relationship better when we wake up.

## Children

Children appear in dreams more than any other family members, and especially our own children. We love them very dearly, but they are also a huge responsibility as they rely on us completely. This means that we can have anxious and sometimes downright terrifying dreams about our kids.

With the media available to us 24 hours a day, and reporting on everything a child can experience in any corner of the globe, it's no wonder that disturbing scenarios featuring our children appear in our dreams. We tend to place our own kids in these situations in dreams because we hope that such things will never happen to them in waking life. The good news about disturbing dreams is that they are the equivalent of a physical detox. If you eat junk food all day, your body will process it and then dispose of it. The last thing you would want is for your body to retain the unhealthy stuff. The same thing applies with the material you have viewed, heard, or read. Just like junk food, you've absorbed it and it needs to be disposed of. It's my belief that dreams are the disposal system for negative emotions, concerns, and fears. In other words, if we see a disturbing story about a child, we react with empathy, followed by anxiety and fear. It's good to keep the empathy, but we want to dispose of the fear and anxiety, so we do this through our dreams. The dream scenarios allow us to depict and live out our worst fears. As painful as they are to see, we can take heart from knowing that we are also allaying of our fears and anxieties at the same time.

Of course, we also have many joyful, uplifting dreams about children, but these are self-explanatory. There's only one point about such dreams I would like you to consider, and that is: Could the child in the dream be you? Is the purpose of depicting yourself as a child to nurture and support yourself in a way that was missing in your childhood? Perhaps, by having "new," positive childhood experiences in your dreams, you will feel happier as an adult.

# DAY 13

# Food

I don't think there's ever been a point in our history when food has been so popular, so that's our topic for today. These days, we socialize at breakfast, brunch, lunch, and dinner. There are countless programs featuring cooking contests and celebrity chefs, and an abundance of cookbooks. Food appears more often than before in our dreams, too, but not just because we're hungry. In the past, dreams of food used to occur in direct relation to its scarcity or availability in our waking lives. These days, food dreams are more about socializing, body image, and celebrity status.

Looking at your dream of food, let's explore the following:

- Who am I sharing a meal with?

- Is there enough food for everyone?

- Is my portion too small?

- Do I like what is being served?

Answering these questions will be a good indicator of how you feel about anyone joining you for the meal in your dreams. If you care to go deeper, you can also find out how you feel about the way they are currently treating you. If there is not enough food to go round, you may feel that your dining companions are not giving you enough credit; if you felt your portion was too small, this could mean that your input into the relationship is being trivialized; and if you don't like the food that is on offer, perhaps it's an indication that their tastes are not the same as yours.

Hippocrates, the father of medicine, said: "Our food should be our medicine. Our medicine should be our food. But to eat when you are sick, is to feed your sickness." Following this hypothesis, it is essential to try to recall exactly what you were eating in a dream. It's worth taking the time to do this because whatever you're chewing on could indicate an imbalance in your body. For example, if you're eating an orange in your dream, are you craving more vitamin C? If you're eating broccoli, does your body require more calcium? Or, if it's red meat, perhaps your body needs more iron. Dreams can give great insights into what will bring your body back into balance.

In your dream, are you preparing food or are you eating food that has been prepared by someone else? If you are preparing the food yourself, are you doing so with passion, creativity, and joy? Or are you whipping up something very quickly just to fill a gap in your stomach. If it's just to fill a need, and this is a recurring dream, it may be a good idea to look at the "me" time you allocate to yourself. Are you exercising enough? Are you maintaining your body properly? Are you spending enough time relaxing? Because, if you can't find the time in your dreams to feed yourself adequately, you might not be looking after yourself properly when you're awake. Similarly, if you are preparing the dream food as a celebration or in a creative way, and you don't do this in everyday life, your dream is asking you to put more time for yourself "on the menu."

At some point in our lives we all require intellectual nourishment. Is the food that you're consuming in your dreams indicating that it's time for you to expand your thinking, your wisdom, and your knowledge? Is it really "food for thought" that you want to chew upon? You may see yourself in a dream eating slowly, savoring every mouthful, digesting the meal at a very slow pace. That's when food becomes thought in your dream and thoughts become food for your mind.

These days a large range of cuisines is available in most towns and cities. We could travel the culinary world without leaving our zip code. The next time you have a dream that features food as part of the scenario, ask yourself the following:

- From which part of the world does the food originate?

- Is it flavorsome or bland?

- Am I enjoying it?

- Is it healthy?

These are very important questions if you wish to decode your dream. It is possible that you have a desire to travel to the country of origin of the food you're eating, or that you have an affinity with the people who come from that part of the world. It's also a great indicator of how cosmopolitan or insulated you have become.

Let's say the food you dream of is a delicious spaghetti bolognese. If this is the case, you may have a desire to go to Italy; if, on the other hand, it's tasty fried rice and black bean sauce, the indications are that you'd prefer to go to China or somewhere else in Asia. Dream food can also be cold, mild, hot, or spicy, which is a great indicator of how you feel about traveling to a particular destination. The place is either going to "leave you cold" or invigorate you, and the dream food is telling you which one it will be. As well as pointing to a destination you may wish to visit, dream food can also expose a place that your sleeping mind *doesn't* think you'll enjoy. If this happens, the food in your dream will not taste as delicious as you expected it to.

Whatever meal you see yourself consuming or preparing in the dream, it's important to ascertain if it's healthy or junk food. There is a saying: "You are what you eat." Consider the food in your dream and ask yourself if you felt healthy while eating it. Are you becoming healthier with each mouthful? Or do you believe you are eating too much junk?

This might be "a lot to swallow" about a simple dream. Many of you are probably wondering how a dream about food can tell us so much about ourselves. Indulge me. Spend as much time decoding your food dreams as you possibly can, because food is so much more than just fuel, it's a metaphor for many needs.

When it appears in our dreams, food has a significance that usually goes far beyond survival—it can show us the recipe for a successful and fruitful life.

# DAY 14

# Celebrities

Today we're going to look at the significance of celebrities in our dreams.

It used to be only in the domain of dreams that we could find instant fame and fortune, but now it's possible and just as easy in our waking lives. There's never been a time in the evolution of humankind when it has been so easy to become a world-famous celebrity. Video and social networking sites on the Internet, such as YouTube, Facebook, and Twitter, as well as the many reality shows on television, can all propel us into the spotlight instantly to give us our 15 minutes of fame, and much more.

What hasn't changed is the amount of importance we place on meeting a celebrity. Is that because we hope that some of the star power will rub off on us? Or is it because by meeting a star we feel elevated to their level?

When you have encountered a celebrity in your dreams, ask yourself the following:

- Did the celebrity give me a warm welcome?

- Did they find me annoying?

- Was it a one-to-one encounter or was I part of a group?

- Did I feel like a groupie?

The answer to these questions is a great indicator of the level of your self-esteem. If you felt welcome or on the same level as the celebrity, your self-esteem is high. But if you felt that the celebrity found you annoying or you were acting like a groupie, you may feel that others are much more powerful than you are. It may be a good time to address self-esteem issues and to develop self-confidence strategies.

If *you* are the celebrity in the dream and you are being asked for autographs, your name opens doors, and you feel super-desirable, perhaps you should ask yourself the following:

- Is this wish fulfillment?

- Do I feel this is going to happen to me one day?

- Do I feel this will never happen?

- Was I pleased to be a celebrity or did I wake up feeling unsatisfied?

- Did I use this position of power for good or did I waste it?

Your answers to these questions will give you a good insight into how you feel about attracting more attention to yourself. It could be that you know deep down you'd prefer to be anonymous and not have the spotlight constantly on you. You could also come to the conclusion that although you desire fame, there's no point to it unless it can be used in a positive way that enriches other people's lives. Fame for the sake of it may be like the Midas Touch—it will take you over if you don't know how to control it.

If you are a celebrity actor or performer in your dream, especially if your performance requires make-up or altering your appearance in some way, answer the following questions:

- Am I happy with who I am?

- Do I need to pretend to be someone else in order to achieve?

- Do I need to use other people's words to sound credible?

- Am I two-faced?

- Who is the real me?

These questions, when answered honestly, will help you to understand your character and the many roles you play in life. We adopt different roles while we're awake for several reasons: we can't speak our minds publicly because of political correctness; we can't say exactly what we feel because we do not want to hurt other people's feelings; and revealing our true selves might put us in danger under certain circumstances. In dreams we don't need to worry about this, but if we see ourselves as actors or clowns, or wearing heavy make-up, it's a reminder that it's important for us to be, and to show, our true selves whenever possible.

The best part of dreaming of a famous individual who is a household name is that our choice of celebrity tells us a lot about how we perceive ourselves and whom we would like to emulate. Of course, in waking life, it's highly unlikely that we are friends with any world-famous stars, so we don't know what they're really like. Our information is gleaned from their appearance, their public persona, and what is reported in the media, so we piece together own image of them, which is really no more than a symbol.

Let's use Arnold Schwarzenegger for an example—
I hope he won't mind; it's all good! If you saw Arnold
in a dream, the interpretation would depend heavily
on the stage he was at in his career. He went from
being Mr Universe, to a global movie star, to being
identified with his role as the Terminator, to becoming
the Governor of California. Subsequently he developed
a comic book character called the Governator and
announced his return to acting. By identifying with
the dream Arnold at a particular point in his career,
you could conclude that you have the ability:

- To change careers and be successful.

- To succeed in different languages and cultures.

- To lead and govern.

- To deal with political situations and leave
  them behind.

As we have just seen, celebrities do not normally appear
in dreams just because you have a straightforward
desire to meet them or to be in their shoes.

Their presence is usually symbolic because they represent the qualities and attributes you associate with them in your imagination—wealth, respectability, outrageousness, free-spiritedness, being uncontrollable, creativity, power, and so on. So it's not the celebrity themselves who is important in the dream, it's what they represent to you. Arnold could symbolize any of the listed abilities and traits at different stages of his life or he could encapsulate all of them if you consider his career a whole.

When you see a celebrity in a dream, it's important that you quickly identify what they represent to you and then relate this to yourself by asking, "Is this how I would like to be? Or is it how I would like to be seen by others?" For example, the presence of Bono from U2 in your dream could symbolize how you'd like to use your own star-power to help fight poverty; Angelina Jolie could signify your wish to be a supermum; Madonna could represent a desire for eternal youth; and Lady Gaga could be associated with a need to be totally outrageous and unpredictable, or she could be there to remind you that you should never judge a book by its cover.

# DAY 15

# Colors and Numbers

Our topics for today are colors and numbers. The great thing about colors and numbers in dreams is that they are, by definition, symbolic. Everybody understands automatically that green signifies "go" and red means "stop;" and that four means "quarters" and 12 means "a dozen." When these symbols appear in a dream, they make it easier to decode.

## Colors

Let's start with a closer look at colors. Sometimes our dreams are in black and white. This indicates that we want to see the message very clearly. We don't want any room for confusion, so we eliminate any colors or gray areas. When the messages in our dreams are more nuanced, we create them in color, because colors can more readily convey our moods and set the ambience of the dream.

Red is associated almost everywhere with passion, heat, energy, and power, whereas green is linked with nature, fertility, life, and moving forward. It is very important when embarking on decoding a dream to try to recall as accurately as possible any colors that stood out for you. Recent scientific research indicates that dreams are mood regulators. We may go to bed grumpy or annoyed, but by the time we're ready to get up in the morning, we feel more upbeat. This is because during the night we recalibrate our mood gradually through the images, experiences, and colors in our dreams, so that when we wake up we can feel a lot more positive than we did before we went to sleep.

When recalling colors in your dreams, here are some questions to ask yourself:

- Was the dream in black and white?

- If the dream was in color, what was the most dominant shade?

- Did the dream feel dull or vibrant?

- Was it clear or grainy?

- How did I feel?

Your answers to the above questions will be very useful in pinpointing the mood of the message in the dream. Here is an example: say you saw yourself walking through a green meadow; you looked up at the clouds and they were also green, and then it started raining green drops. You could ask yourself the following questions:

- Am I "getting the green light?" Is it time to get going?

- Is the "grass always greener" on the other side? Am I feeling that there are greater opportunities elsewhere?

- Am I suffering from the "green-eyed monster" of jealousy? Or is someone jealous of me?

- Is it time to care more about my environment and develop "green fingers?"

- Am I "feeling a bit green?" Do I need more experience in a particular aspect of my life?

In the above scenario green is the dominant color, but how it affects our mood and our waking life depends on how we personally feel about green as a color. Two people sleeping side by side can both see green in their dreams, and one could wake up full of enthusiasm and energy to start an exciting new project (to them, green means "Go!"), whereas the other person could feel it's time to start recycling their old magazines (to them, green is associated with looking after the planet and its resources).

# Numbers

Let's now take a look at numbers. Numbers are unique. There can be two individuals with exactly the same name, two books with the same title, two products with the same name, but they can each only have one number. So, sometimes we see numbers in dreams to eliminate confusion, because numbers are one of a kind.

In a dream containing numbers, the quantity can be just as important as the symbol itself. For example, if you see three houses in your dream, it could mean that you're going to acquire more property because things "come in threes."

It is a commonly held belief in many cultures that numbers have a vibration and energy of their own, and that everybody has a lucky number or a number they don't like. While the number 999 traditionally has positive associations (it is the number you call to get help from the emergency services in the UK), 666 has distinctly negative connotations—this goes back to medieval times, when it was believed that 999 represented heaven, but if you turned the digits upside down, it denoted the other place. Other significant numbers include 8, which in the East is a number of abundance, and 555, which signifies change.

When decoding dreams containing numbers, ask yourself the following questions:

- How do I feel about the number I saw in my dream?

- Is it associated with where I live or work, or any of my phone numbers?

- Is the number my birthday or my date of birth?

- Is it a significant date in history or my life?

- Do I feel I'm "just a number?"

- Do I feel my "number is up?"

The answers to the above questions can help pinpoint the significance of the other symbols in your dreams. If you feel you lack individuality, you may see your dream self as "just another number," or "making up numbers." If, in the dream, your "number was up," from one point of view you might feel dread, but this could also have a literal meaning—that you are "on the up" and things are going to improve as your number is going in an upward direction. Once again, it all depends on the *feeling* you have.

Sometimes numbers in dreams can be reminders of special occasions, such as birthdays and anniversaries. There are many people on the planet who believe that if you understand the vibrations of the numbers you were born with, you can truly understand yourself— the study of the significance of numbers is called numerology. The father of numbers, Pythagoras, said "Man know thyself; then thou shalt know the Universe and God."

Whenever we see multiple numbers, such as 1234, we can view them in different ways. Taking 1234 as an example, at first glance you would notice that the numbers are going upward in a sequence. This could indicate that a situation is building up in your life. But if you follow the rules of basic numerology and add up the numbers (1+2+3+4), you get 10. When you add these two together (1+0) you have 1, so 1234 could really mean 1, which is the number of individuality, strength, and willpower. I strongly recommend that for deeper insights into the meaning of numbers in your dreams, you try adding them in the way described above until you arrive at one single number, and then do some research into numerology to find out what the meaning of that single number could be.

# DAY 16

# Examinations and School

Today we're going to look at dreams of examinations and school.

## Examinations

More than ever before, modern life can seem like one big test, so it's no wonder that examinations appear in our dreams so often. Sometimes we are back at school taking them, sometimes we are at work, but mostly we don't recognize the setting. All we know is that we are being examined, and unless we're the examiner, we don't like the feeling.

Take a look at the context of your dream and consider the following:

- Am I at school, university, or some other formal institution?

- Am I in the past, the present, or the future?

- What is the subject I am being tested on?

- Do I know all the answers?

- Do I feel I have enough time to complete the exam?

Your answers to the above questions will give you a good indication of why you feel uncomfortable or at ease in your dream.

The reason why we dread examinations is usually that we fear we don't know the answers—or worse than that, we don't have time to recall the answers. Often, in waking life, we feel that we can answer questions if we have time to think about our answers; the problem with examinations is that time is a critical element. Going back to the dream, what do you believe you can achieve if you have more time or if you have an opportunity to do more research?

Most examination dreams reflect what's actually occurring in your life at the time of the dream. You may dream of a math exam or an economics exam when your finances need attention. Or you may dream of history or geography exams when you are planning an overseas trip or vacation. A language examination can be a sign that you feel you are not communicating well with someone, perhaps a family member, a friend, or a work colleague.

The purpose of an examination is to assess our capabilities, or to test our skill or knowledge of a given subject. It can also be an interrogation or exploration to reveal the facts, such as a medical examination by a doctor. Ask yourself the following about the examination in your dream:

- What would I like to reveal or expose?

- What would I prefer to keep to myself?

- Which capabilities do I want to have acknowledged?

- What do I believe I have mastered?

It's very important to answer these questions honestly so that you can work out whether your concern requires you to take action or whether it should be dismissed.

Examinations and exposure go hand in hand. The result of an interrogation or an examination leads to the uncovering of information of some kind. Some fact about us is going to be exposed or evaluated. What is it that you do or do not want brought out into the open? Is it "fact or fiction"? Is it embarrassing or annoying? No matter what your answers are to the questions, the dream is asking you to consider whether now is the time to deal with the matters they raise, once and for all.

An examination could also represent self-exploration. Are you putting yourself "under the microscope," continually testing yourself to try to prove you are either as good as or better than someone else? In your dreams you may see yourself competing with a work colleague who did not go to school with you, but there you are in school uniform, both sitting the same test. These are not negative dreams, because testing ourselves or being tested usually makes us stronger. What is bad for us is the stress that we create during the process. Here are some more questions to consider:

- Who was examining you?

- What was the topic?

- Did you complete the exam?

- Did you have a sense of failure or achievement?

The answers to the above questions are indicators of your sense of achievement in your waking life. Sometimes we may feel like we're in a rut and not getting anywhere. But through seeing ourselves tested, we can gain a feeling of release because we know we can expect a result after a test. Upon waking you may feel as though the answer is on its way.

## School

At work we often feel under extreme pressure. Frequently, this manifests itself in our dreams in scenarios in which we are back at school. Have you ever had a dream along the following lines: you are sitting back at your old desk, in a classroom, even though you don't fit well in the seat. You're squashed, your forehead is perspiring, and you're continually looking around the room with dread, waiting for the head teacher, who appears bigger and uglier than he or she was in real life. You then wake up in a cold sweat and wonder what this dream could mean. It's quite simple—performance is everything in the business world, and you feel you are constantly under scrutiny. Your dream is telling you that your whole working life feels like one long examination.

It is very common to find ourselves back at school or a place of learning in our dreams. Sometimes we're with our old classmates; at other times, we're in a new group. There are occasions where we see ourselves at the appropriate age and in our school uniform, and times when see ourselves at our current age. We all love the phrase "the good old days," but we tend to best remember our enjoyable experiences of the past, exaggerating bygone pleasures and forgetting or diminishing the importance of the unpleasant or boring parts. So, whenever we are tired or stressed in our waking life, our mind thinks the best place to retreat to is our good old school days. For most of us, this was a carefree time: lunch was made for us; we were taken and collected from school by our parents; and we were given pocket money. The dream could simply be about a desire to go back to days of minimal responsibility. If your experience in the dream was negative, perhaps involving bullying, a lack of academic achievement, or not getting to kiss your first love in the playground, it could be exposing a hidden desire to go back and fix things. How often have we sighed, "I wish I knew then what I know now"? As Oscar Wilde said, "It's a pity youth is wasted on the young," so dreams of school could be about missed opportunities and a desire to have a second chance.

Examinations and schools are both connected with learning. Perhaps all we really want to do is go on a journey of self-examination. Carl Jung put it so well when he said, "Who looks outside dreams, who looks inside wakes."

# DAY 17

# Relationships and Social Media

I think it would be true to say that we have never had so many "friends" but so few relationships. Everybody wants to join us on Facebook, follow us on Twitter, or watch us on YouTube, but how many of these people have actually broken bread with us or given us a hug? So, today, our topics are relationships and social media.

## Relationships

While every type of relationship we have ever experienced presents itself in some form in our dreams, our current relationships are the most prevalent. Our families, our partners, our work colleagues, and even strangers interact with us during the day, and naturally some of them will feature in our dreams, too. Once again, the most important thing for decoding purposes is not the actual content of the dream, but the emotions you felt during the dream and the lingering effect left when you woke up.

If you have a recurring dream, the message is obvious in that it indicates you need to take action as soon as possible to deal with the underlying problem. For example, if in your dream you repeatedly see yourself waiting, say, at a bus stop, outside a front door, or in a strange location, it is reminding you that someone you're involved with is always late. You can respond by staying annoyed and doing nothing, or by telling them how you feel, or even by quietly moving their watch forward 15 minutes without them knowing! But, the dream will continue to recur in different guises until you address the problem in waking life.

Humans are social animals. We tend to be happy in groups and even happier in our own little cliques. Our relationships can actually define us—it's so true that birds of a feather flock together. When you have a dream about a relationship, ask yourself the following questions:

- Is this about my current relationship?

- Is this about a past relationship?

- Is this about a work relationship?

- Is this about any of my friends?

- Is this about someone who is outside my circle of friends?

Location, location, location is all that matters when it comes to real estate. When it comes to understanding how you see yourself fitting into any relationship, it's all about feelings, feelings, feelings.

Now, ask yourself:

- Did I feel like an insider or an outsider?

- Did I feel I wanted to go back into the dream when I woke up?

- Did I feel I was the center of attention?

- Did I feel I needed to attract more attention?

The answers to the above two sets of questions may shed new light on how you really feel about some of your close relationships and the people in your social circle.

Relationships can be very irritating, because in order to establish them you need at least one or more other people, all of whom have their own opinions and agendas. This can lead to conflict and a need to dominate or control others, or to allow yourself to be dominated or controlled by them. Here are some more questions about your relationship dream:

- Am I trying to change someone? If so, who?

- Is someone trying to change me? If so, who?

- Should I listen, or should I ignore them?

The answers to the above questions will give you an insight into the dynamics of your waking relationships.

It's rewarding to be in a committed relationship and it's also natural to want a relationship to grow, but it can be unnerving when past relationships continue to feature in our dreams. Previous relationships can appear for many reasons, so ask yourself:

- Am I getting rid of old baggage?

- Am I ensuring that I don't fall into the same trap again?

- Do I want to get back with my old partner?

- Do I wish they could see me now?

- Is it that I simply can't let go?

There is always a good reason why we dream of old relationships. Often they highlight issues that we still need to address and in this way they can help us to improve present and future relationships.

We give free rein to our imagination when we are asleep, so it is unsurprising that our dreams are often exotic. Most of us have dreamed of people from other cultures or parts of the world, and even aliens, at some time. Such people could represent individuals who are "foreign" to your circle of friends or the dream could be simply reminding you to take action regarding a cross-cultural relationship. When you dream of people from other cultures or of aliens, ask yourself the following:

- Is there is a culture that I want to identify with?

- Am I dealing with any cultural differences?

- Do I feel alienated in a relationship?

- Am I avoiding someone because they have alienated me?

- Am I alienating somebody?

Your answers to these questions may give you revealing insights about how you feel as a citizen of the world and the planet.

## Social Media

There are more and more reported appearances of spiders and cobwebs in dreams. The obvious connection is that the spider's world is a web and we humans now rely more and more on the World Wide Web (WWW). We maintain many relationships these days over the WWW. Who writes a letter? Who picks up the phone? Who makes a visit? Not many of us these days. As a result, in our dreams, we are seeing more complex relationships represented in the guise of tangled webs and more people appearing as holograms or on smart devices.

The fact that so many of our relationships depend on technology and the devices that support them is why more and more people pop into your dreams than ever before. When we're awake we boast about the number of Facebook friends we have and smile when someone new is following us on Twitter. And anything "hot" and exciting goes viral because we want to share it instantly with our friends.

When social media and technology feature in your dream, ask yourself the following:

- Are my relationships becoming more distant?

- Do I miss intimacy?

- Who would I like to meet?

- Do I prefer to keep people at arm's length?

- Do I regret sharing certain things on social networking sites?

- Am I being stalked by someone?

- Am I stalking someone?

The answers to the above questions will give you an idea of whether you'd like to be more sociable in waking life or be more self-contained by keeping in touch through technology.

# DAY 18

# Conflicts, War, and Sport

Today the topics we are going to examine are conflicts, war, and sport.

## Conflicts and War

Any self-respecting samurai will tell you that they live by the maxim, "I have no principles; I make adaptability to all circumstances my principle." If we all lived according to that philosophy, it would eliminate all conflicts, no one would be prepared to give their life for a cause, and we would all simply adapt to whatever was the best solution to a problem.

There are many situations during waking life that demand we blend in and conform, and even more instances where we have to be like a samurai and adapt. But when it comes to our dreams, we are free to express the emotions that we have taught ourselves to control and repress during waking hours, such as hate, anger, frustration, and so on. In our dreams it is not unusual to find ourselves in conflicts, wars, and battles, and we often find ourselves right in the thick of things. When we are asleep we can also be much more willing to take on antagonists, or be much more forthright or opinionated. In this way our dreams allow us to express ourselves honestly every night, without experiencing the real bumps and bruises we would surely get if we dared to behave in the same way in waking life.

The key to decoding the meaning of conflict and war in your dreams lies once more in the emotions you experienced. After you've explored the emotion that lingers upon waking, ask yourself the following:

- How large was the conflict or battle?

- Who was involved?

- Did I take on someone one-to-one?

- Did I feel I was in the right?

- Was I fighting a lost cause?

The answers to the above questions will help you discover what lies at the root of the problem. In this scenario, it's also very important to look at the setting for the conflict: Was it your home, your workplace, a social environment, a familiar place or an unfamiliar environment? The next things to probe are what caused the conflict and why it arose. Did you have good reason to fall out with your antagonist? Or were you simply fighting to prove a point and to cover up the fact that the other person may have been in the right? The size of the conflict is also significant. If it was a large conflict, ask yourself what the great injustice that has been heaped upon you could be. If only a few people were involved, ponder why you feel the need to control what people think. Sometimes we dream of clashes in the workplace that shouldn't have mushroomed into a conflict at all because they turn out to be based on a silly misunderstanding or a simple difference of opinion. After all, everyone is entitled to their own opinion.

If you see yourself fighting someone one-to-one in your dream, it's vital to see if you recognize the person. If you do, and you have issues with them in your waking life, the meaning is obvious. But if you don't recognize the person, you need to consider whether the scenario could be symbolic of an inner conflict. Ask yourself the following:

• Am I battling with my conscience over something I feel I should or should not have done?

• What is my conscience telling me?

- Do I respect my shadow self?

- What don't I like about myself?

Just as when we see ourselves being chased in dreams, we're often running away from ourselves, so when we're wrestling with someone in our dreams, they usually turn out to be ourselves, too. It's easy to love the "goody-two-shoes" side of ourselves, but it can be hard to come to terms with the shadow side who forgets their partner's birthday, can't stand taking the kids to their activities, and hates eating at their mother-in-law's. Minor conflicts, such as these, come to the surface in our dreams.

The wonderful part about dreams that contain one-to-one fights is that you get to wrestle with yourself, as goody-two-shoes and shadow self roll around trying to dominate each other. Once you can accept that there is no "good" or "bad" side, you will see that they are simply the positive and negative sides of your character personified. One cannot exist without the other, and together they blend in a unique way to make you who you are. If you are familiar with the *Star Wars* sagas, you will know that the most powerful individual in the universe was Darth Vader. Although his dark side dominated throughout the sagas, his positive side finally reasserted itself when he sacrificed his own life for his son, Luke.

## Sport

Today, gladiators and knights are long gone and most conflicts are resolved by common law. One of the few arenas in which your country, city or friends can do battle with their rivals is on the sporting field. Sport has taken the place of battles, and has made conflicts more fun. However, the moment someone started keeping scores, or handing out trophies and medals, sport became seriously competitive.

Whenever you see a sporting fixture or any type of competition in your dreams, ask yourself the following:

• Who am I supporting?

- Why am I supporting them?

- Am I participating or am I watching?

- Am I on the sideline?

- Am I winning or am I losing?

- How confident do I feel?

Clearly, if you can relate these dreams to a team you follow in a particular sport or you are an athlete yourself who competes, the meaning will be obvious to you. However, if you believe that the dream had much wider significance and meaning, reflect whether you feel you are supporting the right team. Or are you envious that all you can do is watch, instead of participating? Is your dream telling you to get off the couch, join a gym, and get fit? If you were not in the team but sitting on the bench as a reserve, could this mean that you feel marginalized in a social or work situation? Or does your dream indicate that you are a sore loser—or even worse, a bad winner? The most successful teams have a game plan, and if they stick to it, they have every chance of winning. Do you lack confidence because you're not sticking to your own "game plan," or are you winning because you're confident and you've thought things through?

If you see yourself as a referee or an umpire in your dream, you are probably stuck in the middle of a conflict between two parties or perhaps you don't care what the two sides think or who is winning. You see yourself as the judge and you believe you know what's right and wrong.

To me, the great thing about sport is that the creed of the samurai applies. A great illustration of this is when your captain wins your team the top honors and then decides to move to another team—your opinion of him or her changes instantly for the worse. Similarly, if a great player from another team, who up until now has been derided by your team's fans, suddenly transfers to your team, he or she becomes your new hero. It seems our opinion of the player is governed solely by the color of the team strip they are wearing, which shows how quickly we can adapt and change our point of view when it is to our advantage.

# DAY 19

# Money, Finances, and Abundance

Today we are going to explore the significance of money, finances, and abundance in our dreams.

The old expression, "Money isn't everything," is really half an expression—the rest of it should be something along the lines of "…but I'd rather be crying in a penthouse suite." Or, perhaps the saying should be: "Money isn't everything for someone who doesn't like shopping," or, "Money isn't everything, but it sure beats what comes second." Because over the centuries we have tried to convince ourselves that money is the root of all evil, we seem to have a strange relationship with money. In fact, money itself is *not* evil, it's the uses we humans have put it to that have given it such negative connotations.

Whenever you have a dream about money or finances, ask yourself the following:

- Do I feel that I have enough wealth or resources?

- Do I feel that money flows into and out of my life?

- Do I feel financially secure?

- Do I feel confident in my financial future?

The answers to these questions will assist you in understanding where you perceive your level of abundance is at the moment. Money is only a piece of paper or plastic—it's our attitude to it that's important. The way you respond to money, both when you are awake and asleep, is very revealing. Do you feel that your money or your income "burns a hole in your pocket"? Or do you believe you are "right on the money" and you have everything under control?

Are you receiving or giving money in your dreams? Is the money "new"—that is, do you feel you've earned it? Or have you inherited it or had it given to you (in which case it's "old" money)?

Here is something interesting to consider: if the currency in your dream is different to the currency you use in your everyday life—for example, if you use dollars every day and you receive or use euros in your dream—this could indicate a desire to travel to a country that uses euros. It could also mean that you wish to get out of a relationship because you want to be "on the open market."

Many of our dreams symbolically reflect our current financial situation—they let us know whether or not, deep down, we feel that we're flourishing. We don't have to see actual money in these dreams; instead, our state of abundance or lack can be portrayed in fruitful or barren situations. Some of the popular symbols of abundance people have told me about include orchids, bowls of fruit, lots of fresh produce ready to be picked, and rainbows (because we know there's always a pot of gold at one end of them). We may even see trees in full leaf, and plants and flowers blossoming, perhaps complete with bees buzzing around to emphasize that life is "as sweet as honey." On the other hand, if we are feeling the financial pinch, we may visualize cold landscapes of ice and snow, arid deserts, incidents in which we lose our purses or our wallets, and even the appearance of the dreaded bank statement full of red ink.

You can learn more by asking yourself the following questions about the dream:

- Did I feel well-off?

- Did I feel "short-changed" by anything that happened?

- Did I feel indebted to anyone or anything?

- Did I feel my situation was about to "turn a corner?"

- Did I experience a change in fortune?

As we have seen throughout this book, feelings are paramount in decoding dreams. But with the topic of abundance, feelings are particularly important because abundance means such different things to different people. For example, while some would feel abundant and on top of the world with only 10 cents in their pocket, others would feel poor and hard done by if their multi-million-dollar property did not reach its reserve price in an auction.

Just as the financial markets are extremely volatile, so our feelings about money, finances, and abundance are constantly changing, too. In view of this, when decoding dreams about financial matters, it can help to pay special attention to the dream layers. Is the dream reflecting your current situation? Is it dwelling on the past? Or is it about your hopes or fears for the future? You only have to compare the titles of two of the Beatles' greatest hits to see how times and attitudes change: *Money (That's What I Want)*, was soon followed by *(Money) Can't Buy Me Love*. At some point in our lives most of us truly believe that money will solve all our problems, but we usually come to realize that it *can't* buy you love and neither can it buy you time. And deep down, we all want more love and lots and lots of time.

The media seems besotted with financial experts analyzing the collapse of banks, the decline of previously stable currencies, and the debts of the financial superpowers. So is it any wonder that our dreams contain more references to money, finances, and abundance than ever before? Let's probe a bit deeper. Ask yourself the following:

- Is my feeling about my finances valid or am I being influenced by propaganda?

- Am I in charge of my own finances or are they under someone else's control?

- Do I feel calm and patient, or helpless and impatient?

The answers to the above can help to reassure you about your finances or dismiss unproductive fears. Warren Buffett said, "The stock market is a device for transferring money from the impatient to the patient." Are your dreams telling you not to fret so much, because you're really in a good place and all that is required is a little patience? I once helped someone decode a dream where they saw themselves in a hospital dressing gown in their bank. They saw themselves as *a* patient, but the symbol meant that they needed to *be* patient.

Here's one final point to bear in mind when decoding dreams about money, finances, and abundance levels. Money gives us something we truly crave: choices. The crucial factor is not how much money is available to us, but rather the number of choices that money can offer us. For example, say you are standing outside a jewelry store admiring a diamond necklace in the window. If you look at the necklace and know that you can't possibly buy it, you will probably walk away feeling dissatisfied (even though you neither need it nor really want it). But if you gaze at the necklace in the knowledge that you *could* buy it if you so desired, you walk away feeling content whether or not you buy it. The only difference is that in the second scenario your wealth gave you a *choice*. So remember that money in dreams can also symbolize choices.

# DAY 20

# Nightmares

Today we are going to delve into the phenomenon of nightmares. Worse than any horror movies in 3D, these highly distressing and usually very vivid dreams can occur at any age and can be very frightening experiences. The word "nightmare" is a medieval term meaning "night demon"—in the Middle Ages it was common to attribute any unfavorable nighttime events to demons.

The reason why we dislike nightmares so much is because they leave us with a sense of fear, dread, and anxiety. However, I believe that nightmares are actually a wonderful gift because they alert us to deep-seated emotions that need to be acknowledged and released.

There are so many things and situations that frighten us or hinder our ability to be productive in the waking world. We try to put on a brave face, but most of us delay dealing with them or avoid them altogether, so our mind finds a place in our psyche in which to bury them. But as with anything that we try to suppress, eventually the problems resurface and this time they appear as nightmares in order to gain our attention.

Upon waking from a nightmare, take some deep breaths to calm yourself, then answer the following questions:

- Was I frightened by a childhood memory?

- What exactly was provoking me and causing me anxiety?

- Was I living in the past, the present, or the future?

- Was I affected by something I've recently seen in the media?

- Was the nightmare triggered by something I ate before I went to bed?

The answers to most of the above questions can help you discover what is troubling you in your waking life. You may not be consciously aware that a particular issue is bothering you, or you might believe that you've already dealt with it, but if it comes up in a nightmare, it's time to face the issue and try to resolve it.

The most obvious cause of a nightmare is something you ate. For example, if you went to bed after eating a pepperoni pizza washed down by a mighty fine glass of red wine, you probably wouldn't be surprised if you dreamed that a great big anchovy was trying to devour you. You may have acid reflux and this could translate itself into a dream in which a fire-breathing dragon was about to barbecue you. There are studies indicating that a clear relationship exists between the food and drink we have before we go to bed and what's on the menu when we dream.

Some of the worst nightmares we have involve dreaming that we're trying to run away from someone or something and we can't move, or feeling "frozen" and unable even to raise a finger. Such dreams are really unpleasant, but they're actually very common and completely normal. There is an area in our brain that ensures we don't run, walk, or move around when we're asleep, because it would be dangerous. We developed this facility millennia ago when our distant ancestors lived in the trees and needed to avoid falling out and breaking bones. People in whom this area of the brain is compromised are prone to sleepwalking. The next time you find you can't run away or you feel stuck in your dream, give it a positive spin and think how this is only a protective mechanism that evolved to keep you safe. But, if you find it recurs frequently, ask yourself the following:

- Do I want to run away from my current relationship?

- Am I stuck in a dead-end job?

- Am I being suffocated or overpowered by someone?

- Should I be standing up for myself and my beliefs?

Often, we can't do anything about the above issues in the short term, but we can take steps to overcome them in the longer term. It takes time to leave a relationship or to move jobs. We have to build up our self-esteem gradually to the point where we have enough confidence to stand up to others or to speak out at the appropriate time. I believe that nightmares are part of the process of developing the courage to do these things.

One of the most wonderful functions of the brain is to keep us safe from harm. It processes zillions of pieces of information all at once and allows us to do amazing things safely, such as driving fast cars, flying airplanes, and walking tightropes. The brain also acts like the world's greatest detectives all rolled into one. Imagine Sherlock Holmes, Hercule Poirot, and Miss Marple living right between your ears. The brain is continuously carrying out a myriad of diverse tasks simultaneously—for example, on a conscious level you could be listening to the radio and writing a shopping list at the same time, while subconsciously you are also monitoring everything going on around you. Once we synthesize all the information we collect and process, our brain uses it to makes predictions and to warn us—we call these premonitions, and they often take the form of nightmares. Here is an example: One day, you see a friend driving very fast up your street; on previous occasions you have noticed the same friend talking on their phone and sipping coffee while they were behind the wheel. Your brain collates the facts and concludes that this person could be heading for a car accident. It then presents this information to you in a graphic nightmare.

It is well documented that wild animals don't seem to be affected by or caught up in tsunamis, earthquakes, or natural disasters. Clearly, they can read the natural signs that occur before such events. We have exactly the same ability, but unfortunately most of us no longer listen to our intuition, preferring instead to rely on our intellect. The one place where we are at one with every other animal on the planet is in our dreams. Our most fearful nightmares about catastrophes and disasters are warnings similar to the deductions wild animals make instinctively.

The next time either you or someone you love has a nightmare, it may be worthwhile reflecting on the positive aspects of this very agitating experience. And perhaps we should banish our fear of nightmares by changing the name to something less frightening, such as *night messengers…*

# DAY 21

# All Things Erotic

If you're a Freudian, every banana or fig has sexual connotations, but if you're a follower of Jung, you will give sensual symbols a more spiritual interpretation. This chapter is not going to get into that argument. In fact, it's not going to delve into guilt, lust, and gratification at all. These subjects are so complex that they deserve a book of their own. What we are going to cover today is the relationship you have with your erotic dreams. Your dreams are as private as your thoughts and as personal as your feelings, so there is no such thing as thought crime, guilt, or consequences.

Let's start with the dreams in which we are making love passionately or sharing intimate moments with another person or group of people. Upon waking, you could ask yourself the following questions:

- Am I truly interested sexually in this person or group of people?

- How did I feel before, during, and after the intimacy?

- Would I be tempted if the opportunity presented itself in waking life?

- Would I never want this to happen when I was awake?

In dreams, we often make passionate love to an individual who possesses a quality that we would like to have ourselves. For example, imagine that for some reason your accountant or bank manager appeared romantically in your dreams. Could this be because your finances are in a mess and you covet the ability to handle money that these professionals possess?

No matter with whom you see yourself being intimate in a dream, ask yourself what is it about them that you find so attractive. By cultivating the missing qualities in yourself, you can start to address issues in your waking life.

We are all attracted to many individuals in our day-to-day lives. They may be celebrities, social acquaintances, or colleagues, so it's not surprising that they also appear in our dreams. One of the most important things to ask ourselves when decoding erotic dreams is why have they appeared *now*? After all, most of these individuals will have been around for some time. Are you going through a period of low self-esteem and are you therefore trying to ascertain whether you are still desirable? Does it build up your confidence to see these people attracted to you? If so, don't feel guilty. We may buy a new outfit, or join a gym, or go on a diet to boost our desirability in waking life, but we still need feedback about how well we're doing. So, it's natural to play out these scenarios while you're dreaming because it's not appropriate or possible when you're awake.

Another reason we have erotic dreams is because we are bombarded constantly with all sorts of sexual images in advertising and the media. Movies and television programs are full of erotic adventures in their story lines. Obviously, these are going to present themselves in our dreams, and usually they are dealt with in some fashion or other before we wake up.

We often dream of being reunited with ex-partners, or with individuals from relationships that are long gone. And we wonder why we dreamed of them, as we thought we were over them. In most cases, we *are* over them, but we dream of them to complete some unfinished business in our mind. We could even be tying up loose ends—the proverbial movie script works when boy meets girl, boy fights with girl, boy makes up with girl, and they ride off into the sunset together. Unfortunately, most relationships don't end so predictably in real life, so we sometimes have a dream to neaten things up, so that we can feel complete.

Another reason why we dream of past partners could be that our current partner is behaving in the same manner as an ex did, and that behavior reminds us of what happened last time. If your current partner, say, forgets to put the garbage out, or squeezes the toothpaste at the wrong end, or leaves their clothes on the bedroom floor, and this was a bone of contention in your last relationship, your ex is appearing in the dream to remind you of how it worked out last time. At this point, your options appear to be: to take out the garbage yourself, get your own tube of toothpaste, hang up the clothes, or to get rid of your current partner! Your dream is telling you that if you don't change, you're going to end up with the same result as the previous relationship, so perhaps it would be best to loosen up and meet your partner half way.

One of the best things about erotic dreams is that when we have properly decoded them, we usually realize that we have no desire to have the experience in our waking life. In fact, most of the time, if you dig deep enough, you will discover that you are only making love to yourself. As Oscar Wilde said, "To love oneself is the beginning of a life-long romance."

While we're looking at erotic dreams, I think it's important to understand why we often find ourselves stark naked in the most inappropriate places. It was widely reported that Catherine, the Duchess of Cambridge, dreamed on numerous occasions prior to her marriage that she appeared totally naked on her wedding day. Of course, this had nothing to do with a desire to get married in her birthday suit, but everything to do with knowing that, from that day forward, she would feel completely exposed under the constant scrutiny of the media.

The next time you have a dream where you are naked, ask yourself the following:

- What is it that I would like to expose?

- What is it that I'd prefer to keep secret?

- Who do I wish to reveal my true self to?

- Have I dealt with a situation and now feel I've got nothing left to hide?

It's important to realize that nakedness in dreams does not mean you have a hidden desire to become a professional stripper or a streaker. Nakedness is a symbol of exposure and bringing something out into the open—it's quite liberating because you are exposing the "naked truth."

# Afterword

## Things You May
## Have Missed

On Day 20, we discussed how our brains act as master detectives to help us decode our dreams. Now, my favorite part in every murder mystery story is the part where the detective gathers together everyone connected with the case who is still alive, and goes over the facts that led him to his conclusions. At that point he highlights things we may have missed as the plot unfolded. To follow are some important points you may have missed as you've worked your way through this book. You will find them very useful in assisting you to reach satisfying interpretations of your dreams, and I strongly recommend that you review them regularly.

- If dreams did not serve a useful purpose, we would have stopped dreaming a long, long time ago.

- We speak in metaphors, but we dream in symbols.

- We match dream symbols to popular expressions and metaphors.

- We wake up from a dream with a feeling, not necessarily with knowledge.

- A dream is like an onion—there are many layers to each symbol.

- We manufacture memory in our dreams.

- We solve problems in our dreams.

- We live out our worst fears in our dreams.

- When your teeth fall out in a dream, go and see a dentist.

- Death is often a symbol of new beginnings and regeneration, not termination.

- When you are being chased in a dream, you are usually running away from yourself.

- When you feel you are falling in a dream, it can mean you feel unsupported in waking life.

- If you want your spirits lifted, you will dream of flying.

- Flying in a dream may reflect a desire to get a bird's-eye view of a situation.

- We give animals human traits and personalities, which they symbolize in our dreams.

- Celebrities represent an image—they are symbols of who we think they are.

- Recount your dreams in the first person and in present tense.

- Consider the relationship between your dreams and a situation that's occurring in your waking life.

- Dreams are only irrational when viewed by the waking mind.

- Our emotions create our dreams; our dreams balance our emotions.

Now that we've journeyed together over the last 21 days, I want you to feel like you've just received your driver's license. And now that you have your driver's license, it's important that you don't fill up the car with all your family and friends and start driving them all over the place. You will end up with "backseat" drivers and distractions, and you will possibly also get lost because of all the different opinions about your driving that will be offered during the ride. Furthermore, your first licensed driving experience could result in you losing confidence, and then it might be a long time before you get behind the wheel again. It's far better to go out on your own as many times as possible and build up your confidence. Then, when you make a mistake, there's no one there to criticize, and if you get lost, you're able to find your way home by using your common sense. So, all in all, when you are newly qualified, it's a good idea to make every journey alone.

This scenario applies perfectly to decoding dreams. Avoid proposing to take all your family and friends on a dream-decoding journey. If, at an early stage, you try to become everyone's dream decoder, inevitably there will be many instances when people don't agree with your interpretations or have different opinions, which could lead you to lose confidence. So start by going on your own individual journeys to decode your dreams. There's no point in trying to become a dream decoding know-all, because there is no such thing—it's all about knowing yourself and interpreting your *own* dreams. So, keep it personal and be the only one who decodes your dreams, because then you will have the certainty and closure you desire.

It's now time to hop into your little car, your new license in the glove box. Off you go, up and down a long and winding road that leads you to your innermost thoughts, desires, fears, hopes, and choices. You don't feel alone even for a moment because you know you are on the right road. A familiar song flows out of the radio—it's Mama Cass reminding you to have sweet dreams till sunbeams find you…

# About the Author

**Leon Nacson** is one of the pioneers of the self-help movement in Australia and was the publisher of *The Planet Newspaper*. He specializes in dream coaching as an author and in his regular media appearances. He is the author of three best-selling dream books.

**www.dreamcoach.com.au**